BARBARA DANISH

WRITING AS A SECOND LANGUAGE

A Workbook for Writing and Teaching Writing

Teachers&Writers

5 Union Square West, New York, N.Y. 10003

The publication of this book is made possible by a grant from the National Endowment for the Arts in Washington, D.C., a federal agency.

Every effort has been made to reach, for permission purposes, the students whose poems and stories appear in this book. In some cases this has proved unsuccessful. The publishers will be glad to hear from any such student.

Danish, Barbara, 1948 –
    Writing as a second language.

    1. English language—Composition and exercises.
I. Title.
LB1576.D234   808′.042′.07   81-5755
ISBN 0-915924-10-2   AACR2

Second printing.

For my parents,
Sophie Danish and Abraham W. Danish

ACKNOWLEDGMENTS

Many people have directly and indirectly helped me formulate the ideas and attitudes of this book. I am happy to have this opportunity to acknowledge them.

I thank the many students with whom I have worked and from whom I have learned, especially those from P.S. 107, Brooklyn; P.S. 50 and P.S. 156, Manhattan; C.S. 211, Bronx; Lynbrook South Junior High School; South Ocean Avenue Middle School, Patchogue; School #87, Indianapolis; and Rio Grande Elementary School, Terre Haute. Overall, these students had a great energy, inventiveness and honesty, and their work constitutes a fundamental part of this book.

I am grateful to the administrators who welcomed me into their schools and the teachers who invited me to work in their classrooms; some I also count as my teachers, particularly Virginia Dolan, Helen Arcuri, Patt Trussell, Hazel Roberson, Joyce Sogluizzo and Mary Ellen Bosch.

Working with Teachers & Writers Collaborative has been an inspiring part of my teaching experience and I thank all of my colleagues, especially Steve Schrader, who gave me the opportunity to work with the Collaborative, Nancy Larson Shapiro, Neil Baldwin and Miguel Ortiz.

The written responses and incisive comments of Mary Ellen Bosch, Linda Cave, Judy Danish, Steve Harvey, Susan Rabiner, Ellery Samuels and other teachers and writers were invaluable in helping me see where I had to think harder.

I thank Sandy Kaufman who helped design a book that would be a comfortable place in which to write.

Joy Johannessen, who copyedited this book, not only marked sentences and phrases that were awkward or unclear, but suggested alternatives that made the intention of a passage more clear to me, and for that I am very thankful.

Finally, I am most grateful to Laura Brown, a generous and exacting editor who balanced my sometimes hasty conclusions and impatience with clear and calm thinking, and who inspired me, always, to work harder.

TABLE OF CONTENTS

THE TEACHING LESSONS   117

ONE TEACHER'S EXPERIENCE WITH WRITING   176

THE WRITING LESSONS

INTRODUCTION

If you are a teacher you have probably come to this book because you are interested in new ways to bring writing into your classroom. Maybe you are looking for approaches that will get your students excited about writing; maybe you want to help them communicate more powerfully or grasp the basic tools of writing. If so, you've come to the right place, because these are just the concerns I intend to address. However, the way I intend to address them may lead you in a direction you had not anticipated, a direction you may even feel reluctant to take.

Because if you really want to bring the challenge and intensity of writing into your classroom, if you want your students to write confidently and with power, the unavoidable first step is for *you* to feel comfortable with writing, to believe in writing. And there is no way for you to do that except by writing yourself.

Once you have experienced the excitement and satisfaction of getting your feelings down on paper, of making a reader discover something you have understood, you will be able to provide the kind of classroom atmosphere in which powerful writing thrives. Once you have experienced the problems all writers face — the difficulty of finding subjects, of trusting an audience with your ideas and feelings, of taking chances, getting stuck, and all the other scary things that happen when you write — you will be prepared to teach writing with more sympathy and confidence than any single lesson plan or whole book of writing ideas could ever provide.

Learning to feel comfortable with writing is not nearly as complicated and frightening as many people think. A safe, encouraging environment where you are not judged and are helped with the real basics — getting something to write about and finding something to say — is half the battle. That is exactly what I have tried to give you in this book, both in the first part, where you will actually write, and in the second part, where I discuss how to establish such an environment in your own classroom. If you do the workbook, if you sit down and actually write, if you are willing for a little while to let go of your assumptions and fears about writing and trust the plan of this book, you will develop the confidence you need to teach writing successfully. You will be better able to help your students through the difficulties they are bound to encounter, and you will know better when they have succeeded. Your own confidence, the excitement of your students, and the improvement in their writing will be the least of your rewards for setting out on the course I am suggesting.

There are other benefits, too. For those of you who have always wanted to write, this book may provide just the opportunity you've been waiting for to settle down and try to express yourselves. And for those of you who have come to believe over the years that writing is your enemy, you may find that you no longer feel blank when you try to write; in fact, you may actually find yourself looking for a pencil, wanting a piece of paper. You may finally get a chance to experience writing, not as a terrible ordeal, but as a magical language in which your pencil becomes an extension of your brain — a language that helps you talk to yourself and to others, a language you can share with your students.

How to Use This Book

I have designed the first half of *Writing as a Second Language* as a workbook. Each lesson in this section introduces a writing subject or a writing technique and consists of prewriting preparation and instruction followed by a ten-minute writing period. The lessons take approximately twenty to thirty minutes: you may spend slightly less time writing; you may spend more. The blank space provided for the exercises is arbitrary and does not indicate an amount you are expected to write. I suggest you do one lesson at a time, one or more times a week.

At the end of the writing period you may want to go back to the prewriting information and reread it in the light of having completed the exercise. You may want to reread what you wrote, or you may want to hold off on that. Do what feels most natural to you. When you read what you have written, notice your reactions. Are you dismayed that the writing doesn't sound professional? Are you uncomfortable hearing the way you put things down on paper? Are you pleased that you wrote for ten minutes? Is there a word or phrase you really like? Noticing your reactions will help you understand your attitude toward writing, and your attitude has as much bearing on your ease in or discomfort with writing as your actual writing skills.

Let me assure you that you are not a failure if you find a particular lesson difficult or feel disappointed in something you wrote. No writer is successful every time she or he sits down to write, and the concepts you will be employing are complex and impossible to master fully in twenty-two lessons. As long as you are working in the spirit of the book, there is no way for you to fail, and you will gradually develop trust in yourself as a writer.

If you find, upon completing the workbook section, that you would like to continue your writing education at an intermediate level, you need only begin again. The workbook lessons cover such basic writing subjects and such essential writing tools that they are inexhaustible. Your writing experience the first time through will enable you to respond to the lessons on a more sophisticated level, with more knowledge and insight.

The Journal

As with any language, you must practice writing if you wish to become fluent. I therefore urge you to supplement the lessons in this book by keeping a journal.

A journal is a personal notebook, bought or made, in which you can write anything: the thoughts going on in your mind, daily events, questions, messages you want to convey but can't say directly, lists of things you like and don't like, memories, poems, stories, feelings, observations. If you're not sure what you want to write about on a particular day, you might even repeat a lesson you've done in this book.

If, on the days you don't do a lesson in this book, you can find five or ten minutes to write in your journal, steadily, without judgment, you will find that your writing and your comfort with writing improve constantly. If you can keep your journal even several times a week it will help you. However, I am *not* saying you *must* keep a journal in order to work in this book.

The Teaching Lessons   The second section contains material addressed to teachers. Here you will find several essays on issues central to teaching writing in the classroom: "The Teacher as Authority," "The Teacher as Critic," and "The Teacher as Evaluator." You will also find an explanation of the structure of the writing lesson, followed by a set of lessons and lesson variations to use in your classroom. These lessons are converted from lessons you will have done in the workbook, so they will be very familiar, and you will already be experienced in dealing with the concepts and techniques they present.

FREEWRITING

Freewriting Exercise
Lovelle Edwards

I notice there's no noise in the classroom. I notice that everybody's writing and knows what they're going to write instead of putting the pens in their mouths and staring into space. I notice Larry writing a lot. Now I know where Larry gets all his ideas—by looking around the class to see what everyone's doing and by looking out the window. I notice the person who wasn't here last week and is here this week is stuck. Should I help him out? No, let him keep being stuck because we all know who he's thinking about. Elsie. We all know who he likes and loves. That girl is alright but she's a pain to all the other teachers. She's almost finished her last page. I see a lot of other people thinking, which is hard for them. A lot are stuck and doing less writing. Barbara, I see you thinking when you should be writing. Let you pen be your mouth and mind. I notice Ms. Perez standing over me breathing on my neck, laughing away. Elsie got her second piece of paper. On to another piece. I notice that my hands are very ashy and dirty. I've got a cramp in my arm for doing all this.

What Is Freewriting?

When you freewrite you write steadily, without rushing, without stopping, without judgment.

You do not worry what to write next: you just keep the words coming onto the paper. If nothing seems to be coming out, you can write about being stuck, or you can write "I'm stuck" or repeat the last word you wrote over and over until you get started again.

If your words are misspelled, you don't stop. If your thoughts sound stupid to you or aren't in order, you don't stop. You don't care about finding the perfect subject, getting a meaning across, making sense, or planning what you are going to say next. If your thoughts are going faster than your hand, slow down and be willing to lose some, or jot little phrases on the side of the paper as reminders.

When you freewrite you are trying to get the words moving from your mind to the paper, freely, unself-consciously, and without inhibition.

Freewriting Exercise
Thelma Wolffe

I'm amazed at the preparation it took to get started on this. Of course I put off the whole thing for a long time, but that's not just for writing, that's me. Now, before freewriting, I had to get cigarettes, ashtray, glass of water, make sure air conditioner was at the right temperature, decide which pencil to use—I don't dare use a pen, no matter what you say. The editor is in me and I have to get rid of her, like any other fear or bad habit. I stopped for a few minutes there wondering where to go with that thought and then realized I wasn't writing. Gee, if I keep writing I might have to get another piece of paper. . . .

Why Practice Freewriting?

What happens when you have to write something? Do you find you have nothing to say? Does the story you had been planning suddenly disappear? Does a blank piece of paper make you uncomfortable: How am I going to fill that up? Getting started and having something to say are two of the hardest parts of writing—and yet, they are the beginning of writing.

Freewriting gives you both a way to begin getting words on paper and a way to see that you are full of ideas and feelings and experiences to write about.

Freewriting works for a simple, unmysterious reason: when you freewrite you are no longer responsible to produce a well-thought-out, well-supported, properly punctuated, "creative," legible piece of writing on the first try. On the contrary: all of your time and energy is spent looking around, seeing and gathering what's around you and inside you, and getting it on paper.

"That sounds crazy!" you may say, thinking, "What if my writing doesn't make sense? What if I don't have anything to write?" Freewriting is scary because we've always been taught: Stay on the track! Say what you mean! Get it right the first time! But we weren't taught that by writers. A writer welcomes the chaos of freewriting, for it provides a means of pulling in ideas and memories and information, of seeing things fit together in a new way. A writer welcomes everything in this chaos—the serious and the silly, the trivial and the powerful—without being sure where it will lead, knowing that this act of gathering material is the necessary *beginning* of writing.

Have you ever criticized yourself as you wrote? "Get a more interesting way to begin." "You can find a more precise word than that." "Are you sure a comma belongs there?" "You know that word is spelled incorrectly." This voice that questions and criticizes belongs to the editor in you. The editor's comments are very useful once you have finished writing. Before that, however, those comments are dangerous; you can become so concerned about editorial problems that you don't have the energy to concentrate on what you are writing. In fact, you often can't get many words on paper because you are worrying about what you are doing wrong. When you freewrite you learn to practice separating the writing stage, the time you spend getting words on paper, from the editing stage, the time you spend revising the content and correcting the grammatical and mechanical problems.

Have you ever struggled for hours trying to write something, only to end up with three sentences on paper, and these still not right? When you freewrite you produce a lot of material. You can pull out the strong parts and throw away the rest.

Have you ever felt that what you wrote didn't *sound* right? Most nonwriters spend their time imitating writing they've read instead of trying to be themselves. Freewriting—the steadiness of writing and the absence of judgment—helps you find your own way of saying things. Your words begin to flow more naturally, evoking more connections, more details. You begin to see *your* interests, what *you* want to write about.

Have you ever thought, "I can't write that. What if my friends or my family read it!" The editor in you is your own personal censor. You must force the editor out and give the writer room if you are going to be able to write. Of course, in the end, you will decide if what you have written is to be shared or crossed out or ripped up, but if you worry about that too soon, if you censor yourself from writing what is really on your mind, you will find that your writing stops. You draw a blank. You think you have nothing to say. When you freewrite you are gathering material, not writing a finished piece, so you really are free.

For all of these reasons — the need to separate the writer from the editor, the need for new information, the need to produce a lot of material, the need to find your own voice and to be honest to your thoughts and feelings — you try to put everything on the paper, steadily, not so fast that you skim over your thoughts, not so slowly that you deliberate over every word. Later you will focus your writing on a subject, but now you have to learn how to freewrite, to write everything. If you're suddenly distracted, write that; you might even try to track down your distraction. If you're thinking about a cup of coffee or a telephone call or your writing — how you're bored or anxious or excited or confused — get it down. If the editor is criticizing you, write down exactly what she or he is saying. Connect with whatever is taking your attention, no matter what it is.

Freewriting Exercise
Ellery Samuels

I wish I had a stop watch or an alarm clock. I wouldn't have to keep looking on the wall to see how much time is left for me to complete this exercise. Barbara, if you can read my handwriting I give you a lot of credit. I can't, nor do I bother trying. Maybe I should have been a doctor when I grew up. Then I wouldn't have to worry, not that I really do, about my handwriting. You know what they say about doctors' writing. I think I hit a blank. I really had nothing to say, or actually what I had to say escaped me. So I'll continue by telling you what I'm doing while writing this. I'm listening on the radio to the Yankee game. . . .

What Might Try to Stop You?

I want to describe some problems you may come up against when you start freewriting so you'll be able to recognize them and you won't let them stop you.

Think for a minute of all the things you've been taught that might get in the way of your freewriting.

1. Stay on the subject; this part doesn't belong here.
2. That's confusing; what are you trying to say?
3. That is *not* a subject for writing.

And think of all the beliefs you may have about yourself as a writer:

1. I'm not a writer. I never have anything exciting to write about.
2. What I have to say is stupid.
3. I want to write poetically, and I come out sounding dumb.
4. Writing bores me.
5. I'm not going to tell personal things about myself — even to a piece of paper!

Depending on your background and attitudes, these are some of the thoughts that may arise when you start to freewrite.

Or you may feel awkward and self-conscious and find yourself wanting to stop. You may think to yourself, "Other people might just write what comes to mind, but I'm going to write something *good*," as if someone were going to read and grade your work. Maybe you'll say to yourself, "This is a waste of time. I'm just writing junk," or "This is stupid. I can already do this," or "What's the use of getting words on paper if they don't say anything?"

What can you do if you find yourself having such thoughts?

Well, remember that the awkwardness makes sense. After all, you're trying something new. You'll soon feel familiar with freewriting.

It also makes sense to write as if your ideas and grammar and spelling will be judged; it's always happened before. But try not to write for someone else's eye. If you find that you are, write down what your editor self is telling you to do. Otherwise you are just inviting the editor to stay, and the energy that should go to writing at this point will go to editing.   Let your *writer's* mind have its own way, or you may find that you're unable to write at all.

It is very possible that you'll write junk, but that doesn't matter. We want to get rid of the idea that we have to get fantastic results every time we write. We need to become comfortable, in fact, with producing junk, with throwing away what doesn't work, whether it is a word, a phrase, a paragraph, or a whole piece. For every page of this workbook ten or eleven pages were written! Remember, we are not trying to write something "good." We are trying to learn to get words on paper, to be attentive and faithful to what we see and hear. The more we can do this, the more likely it is that we will eventually produce a truly good piece of writing.

You might be freewriting already, but don't jump to that conclusion. Often we are not aware of our secret reluctance to digress from a given subject, to let our thoughts lead us. We keep them in line according to some preconceived idea of what is acceptable and what is on the track. We need to allow ourselves to get off the track and see what's there, and to suspend judgment while we are looking. What we find will surprise us: memories we had forgotten, sudden realizations that apparently dissimilar ideas actually fit together, submerged attitudes towards the people, places and objects of our world.

As to the uselessness of getting words on paper if they don't say anything, you're right. It *is* useless—in the end. But you're at the very beginning, remember, learning a new language. As long as you worry what you'll end up with before you've even started, as long as the *editor* is writing instead of the *writer*, nothing will change in your attitude toward writing. "But I don't want to make a mess," you may insist. "I want to do a *good* piece of writing." *Freewriting is not our finished product*. We are not producing, in the end, unedited, out-of-control, chaotic writing. Freewriting is a tool for breaking through years of damage and misconception that have led to our inability to write. It is a tool for getting words on paper, for getting off the track.

When you hear voices telling you to keep to the old way, to stick to the point, to rehearse what you're going to say before you commit it to paper, or to censor yourself, *write down what is going on.* You will begin to see that these editorial voices really do exist, and little by little you will get them out of your mind while you are writing. Give yourself time, though. Trust yourself. Freewriting can't hurt you. It can't take away any of the skills you already have. It can only help you feel more comfortable with writing.

Freewriting will become easier and easier and make a lot more sense as you grow more familiar with it. You'll find that it will become one of your most important tools in writing. When you combine it with the specific skills in this workbook, you will discover that through the natural process of writing and absorbing you are beginning to produce stronger, more daring, more coherent and powerful writing.

Exercise

For ten minutes make your writing a mirror of your mind by writing exactly what is going through it: what you are thinking, planning, worrying about, daydreaming, concerned with, anticipating. Let these things come out on the paper. If your mind feels blank, write about that. If you feel uncomfortable, stupid or bored, write about that. If your thoughts are on something else entirely, go to that. Listen closely to yourself so your writing will truly be a mirror of your mind.

If the editor tries to get you to form a thought before you put it on paper, to go back and make corrections, to stop and wonder what to write, use that as your subject: What is the editor saying? Do you want to talk back?

If it is difficult to begin you may want to address yourself to someone, showing that person what is going on in your mind. Or you may want to begin, "I am sitting here thinking . . ." Reserve your judgment as you write. Write steadily, but do not rush.

FREEWRITING II

Finding Your Source of Energy

Finding your source of energy in writing is a lot like going shopping. Sometimes you know just what you want to buy. Similarly with writing: sometimes you know just what you want to write about. You've got energy and a lot to say. But often when you go shopping you have to try on a variety of clothes. You look in the mirror, searching for the right thing, the thing that really fits. That's what freewriting gives you: a way to shop for what you want to write about.

Freewriting Exercise
Faith McNamara

Calm down a little. If you write too fast you will make yourself so cramped and crazy you'll never settle down to anything. What am I thinking about right now? How ugly T. is. How I don't have anything on my mind. I'm very sleepy. I'm always getting sleepy now when I try to write. I'm hot all over too, sweaty hot, like a hothouse plant. Remember the book A. gave me to read? Where the old man is sitting in the humid greenhouse? Actually, A. didn't give it, he recommended it. All the books he liked he made seem special. That was a gift of his. Other people might recommend a book but A. made a presentation of the recommendation, as if the book belonged to him, or at least the reaction to the book belonged to him, and because you were special you had the privilege of sharing it with him. I think all of us who were attracted to him, for all of his arrogance, had a desire to see life so enhanced, to see interactions, however small, so dynamically charged. . . .

This writer tried on many things as she shopped for something to write about, and she could have chosen any one. She could have written about how it feels to be restless or sleepy. She could have gone on about the person she called ugly. She could have talked about what it feels like to have nothing happen in her mind or to be hot. But she went with an association of being hot, a memory of a person. This turned out to be the thing that fit her best at the moment she was writing.

When we are looking for our source of energy we may find ourselves jumping from subject to subject without making connections, not even finishing sentences, mirroring the mind's activity, its stream of consciousness.

Acknowledging Distractions

How many times have you tried to write something and found that everything *but* your subject kept going through your mind? I'm hungry. I hate writing. This is stupid. What am I going to do tonight? What do I have to do this for? Is the telephone going to ring?

Our attention is undermined by such distractions. When we take them seriously, when we turn our attention to them in our writing, we can often get rid of them if they're preventing us from connecting with the topic we want to concentrate on.

Freewriting Exercise
Mary Ellen Bosch

> The temptation of this kind of writing is to think of what different things I could write about so I know that I have enough ideas to last the five minutes I am supposed to write. Lots of ideas go through my head and I always feel like I will miss out on them and forget to write them while I'm working on the other. That happens when I write a letter. I can't keep up with where my mind goes while I write about one thing. Now I feel stuck about what to write next. The kids are outside playing. I hear them. They are having fun. The dog is dying to be untied so she can run around to play with them. It's good for her to run but she gets away from the house and Talya gets worried that she will be hit by a car. The dog is yelping too much. I will ask Talya to let her loose while they play outside. I wonder if the time is up. I guess if I could write this much in a letter as quickly as this I would write letters more often. But people might find it hard to follow my train of thought. I think my sister writes letters like this.

The interlude with the dog allows the writer to get rid of her distraction and continue to think about her subject.

Sometimes distractions can actually become the source of our writing.

Freewriting Exercise
Judy Danish

> I'm feeling anxious now and I can't place the source. This freefloating feeling is worse than a mosquito bite. Enough of that. Let's move on to something else. What else? I'm looking for something to write about. I see my foot. It's up on a chair because it hurts. It looks like a baby foot — has potential but is nowhere near developed. Actually, it looks wrong — protruding ankle, hollow beneath it, undeveloped heel. With the heel resting on the chair, the rest of the foot just flops in. I hate the way it looks. I hate the way it feels. I hate the way I feel with it. Some people have feet that look okay but I think mine look awful. Do I think feet are ugly because I hate mine? Am I jealous because some people don't care about their feet? I like to walk. I like to feel my feet and legs move. It's exciting to suddenly realize they're doing what they're supposed to do even when I'm not directing. At the zoo I look, talk, laugh and walk all at the same time. Terrific coordination.

In this piece, the writer begins by feeling distracted, not knowing what her subject will be. She goes with a little pool of memories and associations that make the so-called distraction blossom into a subject she can write about with energy and feeling. Did she know what she was doing? How did she know what to go with? Here is an interview with her:

When you freewrite can you feel when you get to your energy?
Yes, once you pointed it out to me, then I could feel it. It was the time I was really depressed and I didn't want to write about it, and then I started talking about my foot, and that's when it started coming out. And when I read it to you, you said that was where I found my energy. I didn't

recognize it as I was writing. Once you pointed it out to me, other times when I've been writing I've been aware when that happened.

How do you know when you've hit your source of energy?

If I'm not getting anywhere I look around to pick something and change subjects. At the point where I find the energy I don't look around anymore. I'm less open to distraction. I have exactly what I'm focused on, and I stay with it until I'm finished.

How can you tell when it's finished?

I can feel when I'm losing the energy or when it's going into something else. I can feel that switch. My mind kind of veers off into another place.

Exercise

In this second freewriting we are practicing writing everything. If you don't hit a subject, that's fine. If everything you write is junk, don't worry.

For ten minutes freewrite. Begin with a specific thing you notice around you or a specific thought or feeling, and go from there. Let your thoughts jump if they want to. Let them leap anywhere they want to go, even if it doesn't make sense why they should leap to *that* place, even if they leap to a dangerous topic. Let distractions come onto the paper. They may become your subject. Ask questions if they occur to you.

Write steadily but without rushing. Reserve judgment on the value of your writing. If the editor starts talking to you, get the exact words on paper!

DIRECTED FREEWRITING

Freewriting Exercise
Claire Findlay

> Today I am here at this writing workshop wondering not why I'm here but how I can be helped to be a better writer. I marvel at people who can express themselves in writing and people who are good speakers. I really believe that they go hand in hand. Since I'm a lousy speaker (my voice), my writing happens to be atrocious. I feel that I write childlike—I never come to the point, my vocabulary is zilch and it all is totally boring. But I want to give it a try since it is such a challenge to me. Oh, to be a good writer. I think—could it happen? Now dancing is what I would really like to do and I feel that if I had had training at an early age I could have mastered the art of dance, but writing—that I can't imagine.
>
> It kills me when I think of things that I can do well. The only thing that comes into my mind is cleaning. Every time I feel that I'm a failure, have a problem, want to feel a sense of accomplishment, I clean. What does that say for me?

If freewriting is like exploring the whole universe, the infinite possibility of subjects, directed freewriting is like exploring a single star, one subject. But a subject can be a big thing. The subject happiness, for example, has many parts, among them memories of happy times, a description of ourselves when we are happy, the things that make us happy.

When we do directed freewriting on a subject, we try to find something about that subject that gets us excited to write. Sometimes this is easy. We have an immediate direction—a particular time, perhaps, when we were happy. Then we simply direct our freewriting to getting on paper everything we can remember about that time and how we feel about it.

Sometimes, though, we don't have an immediate connection to what we want to say about the subject. When this is the case, when the subject is too large or has too many possibilities, we first direct our freewriting to lightly exploring a few possibilities until we find the one that gets us excited to write. We try to bring the subject into focus.

Whatever amount of focusing we need, even if we know exactly what our subject is, we do not abandon the principles of freewriting. We do not start planning what to say or putting things in the correct order before we get them on paper. We do not revive any of the editing habits that made us blank and tense.

We still write steadily, not rushing. We still reserve judgment and write everything, knowing that there will be a time later to cross out what doesn't make sense. We still acknowledge distractions, and we may even go with them a bit to see if they tie up to our subject or to try to get rid of them. We still adjust our writing until we connect with an energy.

The only difference is that we tighten the focus. We are moving in a space that has boundaries.

Exercise

For ten minutes direct your freewriting to the following subject: You and Writing. This is a large subject, and in your wanderings to connect to your source of energy you might go through, or be immediately attracted to, some of these questions:

1. Do you have specific memories about learning to write?
2. Do you have specific memories of being successful at or proud of your writing?
3. Do you have specific memories of failing or feeling uncomfortable because of your writing?
4. What goes on in your mind when you face a blank piece of paper?
5. How do you feel when you work in this book?
6. What do you hope to accomplish by working in this book?
7. How are you feeling right now about writing?

You may find yourself interested in a category that isn't here. That's fine.

You may find yourself jumping from one category to another, trying to find your source of energy. No problem.

You may not find your source of energy. That happens.

Remember, you are still freewriting, even though you are exploring a single subject. Let everything move from your mind to the paper without deciding what's important and what isn't. Don't force yourself into a subject; allow yourself to find your connection. Your goal, still, is not to write something acceptable. It is to practice using freewriting in a directed context.

You may want to begin, "I am sitting here . . ."

THE FUSS OVER DETAILS

A detail is concrete. It is a fact. You can see it or smell it or touch it or taste it or hear it. We perceive details through our senses. We take these bits of information and collect them, categorize them, arrange them, analyze and evaluate them, and arrive at conclusions, points of view. The latter are generalizations and interpretations, and they are abstract. They are built on details.

We may say a sound is horrible, but we can't *hear* horrible. That is an evaluation of what we hear: fingernails scratching down a blackboard, a car alarm whining on and on.

We don't taste *food*. That is a collective word for specific things we eat: chilled cantaloupe, chocolate ice cream, a salted pretzel.

Nature, too, is a collection or category that we can't hear, smell, touch, or taste. What we can smell is cut grass, evergreens, roses, mildew.

Aristotle says, "There is nothing in the intellect that is not first in the senses." We continually receive sensory impressions, details, from which we build likes and dislikes, conclusions and ideas.

Since this is how we come to know things, writing tries to approximate the same process. But writing has a disadvantage. It is *not* the concrete experience. It is a series of words, marks on paper really, that tries to get a mind to start working: imagining, feeling things, reliving actual experiences.

The fuss over details compensates for the disadvantage of having no actual experience in the written word. When we fuss over details, we are giving the mind specific suggestions about how to get activated, how to fill out abstract words with concrete sensations. The more detailed our suggestions, the more actively we prod our minds or the minds of our readers to get busy reliving tastes, textures, sights, smells, and sounds. Our words take on concreteness and meaning.

In the following list, underline the word in each line that you can *more exactly* see, hear, taste, touch, or smell — the one that really activates your senses.

1. loud   clap of thunder
2. chocolate   sweet
3. elephant   big
4. somberness   hushed voices
5. sharp   razor blade
6. bungalow   house
7. tree   weeping willow
8. pungent   rotten egg

Now look at this paragraph. Try to be aware of how many senses are activated by the writer.

In a Gym
Scott Stein

I am in a gym lifting weights. I smell the sweat of the men working out. I love the sound of weights and barbells hitting each other and clanging together. It looks like an entire army of people pushing things up and down, backwards, sideways, all around. It has pictures of body builders competing against each other. There are weights, weight lifting equipment all over the room which is very bright and noisy.

The sound of barbells clanging, the smell of sweat (and even the implied salty taste of sweat), the picture of people moving energetically together — all are concrete details that conjure up the actual world of the gym and provide evidence for the writer's conclusion that the gym is a bright, noisy, wonderful place.

Exercise

What are the concrete details that you see, smell, hear, taste, or touch around you at this moment? For ten minutes direct your freewriting to collecting these details.

If you find yourself writing, "This apartment is really shabby. I hate it," pull yourself back to a specific part of the room — a wall, the ceiling, a particular chair or pile of papers — and see and record the precise details that cause the room to appear shabby.

If you find that a detail touches off a memory, look at the memory through concrete details.

If you have a distraction, don't censor it. See where it goes. If it leads you away from details, pull yourself back to where you are right now, to the sensory stimuli around you.

Don't worry about making sense or getting things in order or covering all the senses or making transitions.

Relax. Don't edit. Don't rush, but write steadily. Just talk to yourself and point out all the concrete details around you.

BRAINSTORMING

When we brainstorm we make lists. We gather as many ideas as we can, quickly and without judgment. The absence of judgment helps us combine ideas in new ways, suggest possibly outlandish (at least at first sight) ideas that pop into our minds, remember things we may have forgotten, and say things that do not fit at all.

Besides relying on absence of judgment, brainstorming relies on time. Our initial responses to a problem are often the most familiar ones. If we push on we find that one idea suggests another and our minds get limber and more daring; they take chances. Ideas come up, and we aren't sure where they came from. We're surprised we know so much.

When our brainstorming is finished, we can evaluate what we have. Once we have a lot of material we are able to compare and make selections.

In this workbook we use brainstorming in several forms. We have already been freewriting, which is a form of brainstorming, and now we will practice listing, to help us find subjects and gather details. However brainstorming is used, the principles remain the same: reserving judgment and taking time.

Brainstorming Places

Many times we feel we have nothing to write about when the real problem is that we don't know how to tap into subjects that are important to us. One way to deal with this block is to brainstorm lists. Here we have chosen to work with the general category of *place*, but it could as easily be *people, objects*, etc., and the technique would be the same.

Take a few minutes to brainstorm a list of places you've been. Don't rush, and don't evaluate or censor your ideas. Just list any place you've been that comes to mind. Make those places specific. If you write New Orleans, for example, also list specific parts of New Orleans. If you remember the zoo, list specific areas of the zoo.

Here are some suggestions that cover a wide range of places. If you run aground in one direction, one of these categories might help you go off in another direction. Visualize the place in your mind; that often works to trigger more ideas.

> Think of specific places in your house;
> places out of doors — places with sand or marshes or cliffs;
> stores, schools, jobs;
> secret, dangerous or peaceful places;
> places you've known very late at night or very early in the morning;
> a highway, a street, a path;
> a place you knew when you were very young.

_____   _____

_____   _____

_____   _____

_____   _____

_____   _____

_____   _____

_____   _____

_____   _____

Look over your list and star a few places you have a feeling for, whether it is positive or negative. Now circle the place you'd like to consider in more detail. This is your subject.

You have just used brainstorming to find a subject, and now you are going to use directed freewriting to gather details within that subject.

Exercise

Put yourself in the place you have chosen—not in an event that happened in that place, but in the place itself. For ten minutes direct your freewriting to describing that place in *present tense*, as if you were there now. For example, "I am sitting on the steps looking down to the basement. It is dark except for the crack of light under the door. . . ." If you find that writing in present tense is taking a lot of your concentration, write in the way that feels most comfortable.

Notice in your writing everything around you: objects, people, the weather, light and shadows, colors. Are there specific sounds nearby? Far away? Are there conversations? Quietness? Are there specific smells? Textures? Tastes? Do you see any actions?

Don't worry about writing in order or writing well. For now there is only working towards being able to get the words easily and naturally from your mind to the paper without feeling there is something you *should be* writing.

Write steadily, without rushing, without stopping, acknowledging distractions and then pulling yourself back to the place you are in. If you're not sure how to begin, you might start, "I am here . . ."

GOING OUT ALONE

Writing is a process that consists of many parts: getting words on paper, finding a subject, discovering what you want to say about the subject, learning techniques of making the language more concrete. In the previous pages we've been exploring these parts of writing. You may not feel comfortable and successful yet in what you're doing, but you have begun to be able to freewrite, to direct your freewriting, to brainstorm and break down a large category to find a subject, and to use concrete sensory details.

But there is another part to the writing process, and that is using those techniques to go out alone into writing.

Every so often in this book I will give you a place to go out alone if you want to and if you feel courageous. You have certain tools already, and they will help you find a subject and write about that subject: you may want to repeat a lesson; you may want to freewrite, beginning from specific objects you see around you or from a specific idea or feeling; you may take a subject you've been thinking about and direct your freewriting toward it. Whether you choose one of these approaches or another subject that interests you, the principles of freewriting and emphasizing details will always help you.

On the other hand, if just reading this makes you nervous, turn the page fast! You can always come back later.

Exercise

For ten minutes write steadily, reserving judgment.

FOCUSING YOUR SUBJECT

Sometimes when your focus is too broad all you can write is a generalization:

My Life as a Teacher
Kay Levinson

> I've had a reasonably good career as a teacher. Some days have been good, some bad. The first years were hectic, then they calmed down. I finally got all the materials I needed and then I didn't have to spend all that time hunting around for them. I have to admit I sometimes thought I should quit but then I didn't think of a job I liked better so I stayed.

This piece of writing covers so much time and so many feelings that it ends up showing no time. It lists categories—good, bad, hectic, calm—but does not really make us *feel* what it has been like for this person to be a teacher.

One Time in My Teaching Career
Ellery Samuels

> This looks to be another crazy school year. Maybe even crazier than any of the twelve in the past. Actually, my first term teaching was probably more intense than anything else. But that was so long ago. I remember my first days in school. Here I was, a white boy from Flatbush with little or no real contact with blacks before, thrust into a classroom with no practical teaching experience behind me. I remember walking into J.L.'s fourth grade class to give a Language Arts lesson. I was prepared and scared. Thirty children were in their seats. I had been teaching for all of thirty seconds when Lenora and Diane (I'll always remember their names) started mouthing at each other. "Your mother," etc. I tried to get their attention but they weren't having any of that. They were ready to fight and there was no stopping them. They were on the floor, punching and kicking, scratching and biting. The class had surrounded them and was urging them on. And then it happened. Diane grabbed hold of one of Lenora's braids and pulled it, red rubber band and all, right out of her scalp. Well, there wasn't a sound to be heard. Diane was standing there staring at the braid in her hand like an Apache holding a scalp of a cavalry man. Lenora was not in pain but was too dumbfounded to say or do anything. I certainly didn't know what to do. The class just shut up and stood. I don't remember what happened next but I'll never, forever, forget that incident.

In this piece the author has provided us with a concrete time: we can see his nervousness, the classroom, and Diane pulling Lenora's braid right out of her head. We are dumbfounded along with the rest of the class. When a writer focuses on a particular time, he is able to show the exact situation and convey a feeling.

How do we focus a time so we can find and present details? We make sure that we are dealing with a *specific time* in a *particular place.* For example, if I want to write about the time I went to St. Louis I will find that time too broad as soon as I start writing about it: "We left early in the morning, and we got to the city, and then we went to find a motel, and finally we got to the art museum." I need to *break down* the time in St. Louis to its specific parts: going over the bridge into the city, standing at the edge of the Mississippi River, eating dinner on a riverboat, seeing the painting exhibit. Once I see the separate parts, I can pick the one that pulls me to it, the one I respond to and want to spend more time with. Right now I think I would choose going over the bridge or standing at the edge of the Mississippi. I would begin writing from one of those places — *in the car* or *at the river* — and I might start with a detail like "Driving over the bridge into St. Louis with my friends, the radio turned up loud and all of us singing, I suddenly felt as if we were in a movie."

If I think about moving to my new neighborhood I realize that time is made up of particular memories: getting lost riding my bike, my sister's first birthday party, my mother registering us in the elementary school. When I begin my writing I will start *on my bike* or *at the party* or *walking into school*.

If we try to cover too great a period of time we will lose the details, and the details are what make a piece exciting to read — and to write. There is no hard-and-fast rule stipulating how long or short a time period has to be in order to work. Maybe you can combine two times. One detailed sentence might be able to represent a day passing. The only rule is that the subject must be focused enough to capture the specifics that will give a clear picture *on the paper*.

In order to get a subject and practice focusing, you are going to brainstorm pleasant and not-so-pleasant memories. Take your time. Notice how specific words trigger memories. If a memory unrelated to one of the following suggestions comes to mind, write it down. If you don't have enough room, use the empty parts of this page. Brainstorm *specific times* you remember being alone: in a bedroom, in the water, at a dance, near the trees, etc. If you remember an extended incident — traveling across the country, for example — break it down into more specific memories.

_____   _____

_____   _____

_____   _____

Brainstorm specific times you first learned to do something: ride a bike, skate, cook, shave, set your hair, play the piano, etc.

_____   _____

_____   _____

_____   _____

Brainstorm specific times when you were the center of attention, times you were in charge: at camp, at a party, in a classroom, in your family. Include any other memory that comes to mind.

_____   _____

_____   _____

_____   _____

Brainstorm some other categories—for example, times you had strong emotions
—and then break them down into specifics, for example, times you were sad,
etc. Visualize yourself to help get a memory. For example, see yourself sad and
let your mind fill in the details of where you are and what has happened.

_____   _____

_____   _____

_____   _____

Look at the specific incidents you have gathered by brainstorming. Check a
few you feel strongly about, whether your feeling is positive or negative.
Of these, circle the one you'd like to work with. This is your subject.

Exercise

For ten minutes direct your freewriting to this subject. In what specific place does this memory begin? Do
not give background, just jump right in where the memory starts. If you find yourself writing a list of
generalizations—"We went to the movies, and when we were finished we went to have ice cream. After we
got home . . ."—stop. Choose one of those times to see *in detail*, one that starts in a particular place.

Notice all the concrete details of that time: how people move, sounds, conversations, particular smells
and textures, particular thoughts going through your mind. As you write, see the event in your mind as if it
were happening now, and write it as if it were happening now, in present tense. For example, "I am sitting
in the kitchen . . ." If writing in present tense takes too much of your concentration, write in the way that
feels most comfortable.

Remember that you are still freewriting, although you are directing your freewriting to a particular
subject. Don't forget to write steadily. Do not rush. Do not edit yourself as you write. If you begin with
one memory and another one wants to be written about, either save it for later or go with it; see which
memory is the source of your energy.

SHOWING VERSUS TELLING

Although we tend to speak in generalizations, these generalizations are based on precise details we have consciously or unconsciously observed. We might generalize that it is a beautiful day, but we base that conclusion on the evidence that the sky is a brilliant blue, the sun is warm, the breeze is cool. In writing, the power and truth of a generalization or idea comes from what it is based on — the details.

Let's say we're watching a TV show together. We're both taking in details. We see the main character sneering. We hear him tell his supposed best friend a lie. We watch him setting up his partner. During the commercial you say, "That guy's a monster" — a generalization. But since we've shared a common set of details I know exactly what you mean. And if you had been writing this TV show down as a story and you presented, *showed* me, these details, I would draw the same conclusion when I read it. In fact, *you wouldn't even have to tell me he was a monster.* When the details are clear and precise, they lead us to conclusions.

This process is at the heart of writing. Even if you don't create a shared set of details, a common experience, between you and your reader, even if no one ever reads what you write, showing versus telling is still important because it allows *you* to discover what you feel. Details are so strongly at the base of our conclusions that often, if we don't know what we think about an experience, a person, a place, just focusing on the details can reveal it to us.

In this lesson we are going to cut out the generalizations entirely so we can see the details more clearly. For now, no abstractions, no interpretations, no conclusions — only concrete details.

In each pair of sentences that follows, one sentence *shows* action or physical fact, and the other interprets or *tells* action or physical fact. For each pair of sentences check the one that shows.

_____He was surprised.
_____He opened his eyes wide and clapped his forehead.

_____She charged across the street shaking her fist.
_____She was mad.

_____She hated that sound.
_____Her shoulders shot up toward her ears, and she winced.

_____His leg hurts.
_____He limps down the street.

The following sentences show a physical fact. For each one write a generalization that interprets or *tells* the fact.

The dog yelped and ran in circles.

The sun filled the air and sparkled on the leaves.

_____

She sank into a chair and yawned.

_____

The following sentences *tell* or interpret a fact. For each one write a sentence that *shows* instead.

It was a nasty day.

_____

The child was ashamed.

_____

The room was clean.

_____

Write a generalization that *tells* one feeling you have about the place you are in. For example, "It is pretty," "It is a mess," "It is enormous," etc.

_____

List details/facts about this place that *show* or support that generalization.

_____

_____

_____

A camera is an instrument that can't make interpretations. It can only record details. Sometimes a simple technique like pretending you are a camera can help you avoid generalizations. Here is a writer watching herself as she works in this book:

Directed Freewriting
Mary Ellen Bosch

> Her left elbow is on the table leaning on the left hand page. Her left hand is holding her head up. It is touching the tip of her forehead. Her fingers curl into her hair. Her right foot touches the floor. It bounces up. When she pauses, sometimes her toes move up and down.

Here is a writer watching someone else as he watches television and eats.

Directed Freewriting
Linda Cave

> Bob is sitting in an orange recliner chair watching TV. His right leg is crossed over his left leg with all ten toes pointing to the white ceiling. His right hand is in a relaxed position with the fingers hanging over the arm rest. The left hand is in a fist position. Now it is moving to the lips which are moving up and down. As his lips move, so does his right ear that I can see. The jaw is powerful as the skin flexes tight, then relaxes. His right fingers scratch his leg, now are rubbing his mouth. He just smacked his lips. His left toes are wiggling in a slow motion rotation.
>
> The face just twisted to push the food around. The head is turned toward a TV. Interest in the program has stopped the chewing process. His eyes are staring as if deeply interested in what is being viewed.

Exercise

For ten minutes direct your freewriting to describing yourself as you do this workbook or describing someone else in the room as they engage in a particular activity, no matter how small — even something so simple as watching television. Record the action as a camera would, just as it is happening right now (present tense). Even if you are writing about yourself, watch yourself objectively (third person: "She leans on her hand," etc.).

Pay attention to the smallest detail: gesture; position of feet, fingers, mouth, back; sounds.

VERBS

Listing Verbs

Start listing verbs.

_____ _____ _____

_____ _____ _____

_____ _____ _____

Keep listing verbs. (Have you thought of ways the toes, arms, ears, etc., move)

_____ _____ _____

_____ _____ _____

_____ _____ _____

Continue listing verbs. (How about breaking verbs down? For example, you can break _talk_ down to "mutter," "chatter"; you can break _eat_ down to "chomp," "nibble"; you can break _destroy_ down to "smash," "rip.")

_____ _____ _____

_____ _____ _____

_____ _____ _____

Don't stop listing verbs. (Think about movements you make when you're angry, nervous, bored.)

_____ _____ _____

_____ _____ _____

_____ _____ _____

Let's give it a _real_ try—listing verbs. (How about visualizing a story, a series of actions. What happens next? Next? Next?)

_____ _____ _____

_____ _____ _____

_____ _____ _____

Finish listing verbs. (Let your mind go wild! Make wild associations! Leap from verb to verb!)

_____   _____   _____

_____   _____   _____

_____   _____   _____

Are you surprised at how many verbs you found? Is there a verb for what you'd like to do to me right now? Just kidding. (There's one — kid, joke, poke. Stop. STOP!)

Using Verbs to Show Facts

Verbs are powerful tools for showing facts. Compare these sentences by visualizing them as you read:

> Paul had a hamburger.
> Paul gulped down a hamburger.
> Paul picked at a hamburger.

All three sentences tell us Paul had a hamburger, but the last two give us more information because of the verbs they use. In the second sentence we read the word *gulped* and see someone in a rush, getting the eating over with as quickly as possible. In the third sentence the word *picked* gives us an entirely different movement. Whether Paul is looking for something in his hamburger or just isn't hungry we don't know, but he's definitely not in a hurry.

All verbs show an action, tell a simple fact (consider verbs like *go, see, understand, explain*). Some also give us a picture (*gulp, pick, throw, crawl*). Some are even more intense. These are the onomatopoetic verbs, verbs whose sound actually imitates the actions they describe. In fact, the sound seems to *be* the action itself (*click, crack, screech, whisper*). If you say these words out loud, enunciating very clearly, you will be able to hear them sound like the actions they describe. (You might want to go back to your list and see what different kinds of verbs you have included.)

So, verbs can do more than describe an action. They can also give a visual image, and the more intense can give, in addition to a picture, a sound. These sounds and pictures make our sentences more concrete and richer.

In this section we are going to work on seeing how verbs can be powerful tools for showing facts.

In the following sentences, what information might we be getting in addition to the fact that *Shirley wore her new shoes*?

Shirley limped in her new shoes.

Shirley clattered down the street in her new shoes.

_____

In the following sentences, what information might we be getting in addition to the fact that *the car was going down the street?*

The car tore down the street.

_____

The car rattled down the street.

_____

Sometimes you can have two verbs that are very close in meaning, and yet one has the precise shading or nuance you need for your sentence. In the following sentences, what different shades of meaning can we get in addition to the fact that *I didn't talk to her at the party?*

I ignored her at the party.

_____

I snubbed her at the party.

_____

In the following sentence, replace the verb *went* with a more active verb that leads to a different, more specific interpretation.

I went to the store.

_____

Now in the following sentence replace *moved* with a more active verb that leads to a different, more specific interpretation. Try several substitutions and see how the sentence changes each time.

The tree moved in the wind.

_____

_____

_____

Directed Freewriting
Faith McNamara

> Outside the streets are noisy. There is a demonstration by a small but loud group of people saying "Boycott!" K. goes up to one of them and is offered a pamphlet calling for a boycott of all downtown stores. In front of the department store a group is saying "Don't buy. Boycott! Don't buy. Boycott!" Two boys have set up playing congos. Other boys and men have made instruments from building materials which are lying on the half-finished street mall. One plays the top of an industrial barrel, another hits a pole rhythmically against a wooden board, while a third plays the long drain pipes lying on the street with a short metal rod. The street is full of shoppers and police. Many onlookers are moving to the music which is rich and intricate and lively. K. and I leave reluctantly, feeling too reserved to join in but wishing we could.

**Making Your Verbs
Work for You**

This writer is describing a scene filled with sound and movement. But has she conveyed her impressions as accurately and powerfully as she could? Look at the paragraph again.

> Outside the streets are noisy. There is a demonstration by a small but
>   shouting
> loud group of people ~~saying~~ "Boycott!" K. goes up to one of them and is
>   demanding
> offered a pamphlet ~~calling~~ for a boycott of all downtown stores. In front
>   chanting
> of the department store a group is ~~saying~~ "Don't buy. Boycott! Don't buy.
>
> Boycott!" Two boys have set up playing congos. Other boys and men have
> improvised   scattered
> ~~made~~ instruments from building materials which are ~~lying~~ on the half-
>   drums   thunks
> finished street mall. One ~~plays~~ the top of an industrial barrel, another ~~hits~~
>   clangs
> a pole rhythmically against a wooden board, while a third ~~plays~~ the long
>   thronged
> drain pipes lying on the street with a short metal rod. The street is ~~full~~
> with
> ~~of~~ shoppers and police. Many onlookers are ~~moving~~ to the music which is
>   stamping
>
> rich and intricate and lively. K. and I leave reluctantly, feeling too
>
> reserved to join in but wishing we could.

In this revision, the writer has changed the verbs to help her readers hear the music and see the movement. Her substitutions are much more active, and this activity makes the scene come alive on the page.

Avoiding Extremes

Verbs are essential to the energy of a piece. However, if we rely on them too much, our writing can get overloaded and we can overpower the reader. In the above paragraph, for example, we may prefer a verb like *moving* to one like *stamping* because there is already enough sound and activity in the other sentences. Once we become aware of the power of verbs, we need to practice using them so that they contribute to the total picture rather than overwhelm it.

Unfortunately, there is no hard-and-fast rule. I use two criteria: what does the sentence sound like? (Does it sound complicated and overloaded?); and what is the picture the sentence gives? (Is it accurate?). For instance, in describing a conversation, a little goes a long way. Too many intense verbs can make a scene overly dramatic, so that the entire piece can't be received. For example,

"I called it first," I growled in anger.
"Too bad. Go in the living room," he thundered.
"I can't," I whispered.
"Why?" he snarled.

Exercise

Look back at the verbs you listed at the beginning of this lesson and let them trigger memories for you. For example, if you put down *break*, visualize something breaking. What is it? Let your mind supply more details until you can see it clearly. Daydream the memories until you come to one that claims your attention, one you want to write about. It may be funny or serious, momentous or ordinary. If you find that several interest you, choose the one you remember most vividly. Once you know what memory you are going to use, think about the feeling or emotion connected to it.

Now, as if you were a camera, as if this event were taking place right now and you were watching it, record the memory in the present tense or if that takes too much of your concentration, in the past tense. If you want to, write about it as an objective observer, in third person ("*She* sits/sat down").

Remember that you want to show everything: yourself and the others who are in the memory; precise actions, speech, gestures, facial expressions; the environment that is important to this memory.

When you finish writing, go back and reread what you wrote. Does it capture the emotion or feeling of the memory? Look at the verbs. Do they help convey the feeling? Do you need to go back and change any of the verbs to make the feeling more precise? Remember, consider these questions *after* you have finished writing.

For ten minutes direct your freewriting to recording what happened. Write steadily, without rushing; reserve judgment.

THE WAY YOU SOUND ON PAPER

Freewriting Exercise
Mary Ellen Bosch

> If I didn't have a cold I would be able to smell the cakes that are in the oven. They will look good when they are done. One round one and one oblong one. What is the next thought in my head? I am thinking to pick and choose and to discard some thoughts that only come to me in phrases. They don't count because they have to be thought about more to come out right. I hear lots of sounds and it is strange to me to be acutely aware of the ideas in my head and at the same time to be recording the sounds that are around me. It is like being on two separate levels of awareness. Do these sounds get put away in our minds to come out later? Do they help with or interfere in the process now of writing my thoughts?

Freewriting Exercise
Ellery Samuels

> My wrist hurts. If I knew I would have to keep on writing I might not have started this section. But, be that as it may, I will continue freewriting. You know, people pay analysts a great deal of money for the same thing I'm doing now. Reggie Jackson just hit his 33rd homerun of the year. He's so good. Anyways, for fifty bucks a person can ramble on and on like this and an analyst, psychologist, therapist, etc. can get rich. Are you sure you're in the right profession? Maybe I should be lying down while writing this. If I did my MontBlanc fountain pen wouldn't work and you'd have nothing to read. But then again after reading this you'll agree you still have nothing to read. That is, if you can read it in the first place.

In writing, *voice* is the term we use for the way a piece sounds. The voice of a piece of writing is the voice of the writer. Can you hear the different voices in the two passages above? The first sounds very serious. The second sounds playful. Both sound like the writers are speaking in a voice they are comfortable with, one that comes naturally to them.

Nonwriters often spend their writing time doing just the opposite: mistrusting their own voices, they try to imitate the way they think writing *should* sound, the way books they've read sound. Sometimes they do this because they're convinced that there is a *correct way* to write. Sometimes they're afraid they have nothing to say, or nothing anybody would want to hear. They figure that if they imitate what worked for someone else it will work for them. So when they write poetry they try to sound "poetic," using *thee*s and *thou*s and *beloved*s and inverted phrases: "Love I your precious face." When they write essays they try to sound authoritative, using words like *furthermore, nay,* and *to wit.* When they write about life they try to sound profound, using big concepts like Truth and Righteousness. They resort to such tactics even though what they end up writing doesn't sound at all like the way they talk. In fact, they're often so concerned about getting the *right* sound that what they write doesn't make sense:

Subway graffito

> We all have an inner mission in life
> either to live or die
> laugh or cry
> fail or succeed if we all try.

Because they concentrate on imitating someone else's voice they never get around to describing what happened to them, don't connect with their subject, and grow bored or feel stupid. That's when they protest that they knew all along they weren't writers and weren't creative and didn't have anything to say.

Imitating someone else's voice is like presenting someone else's experience as your own. Your writing is bound to sound self-conscious, awkward, and empty, just as you are bound to feel self-conscious and awkward when you allow yourself to be nothing more than an imitation of someone else.

You can't talk about the important things in your life, and you can't figure out what those things mean to you, by being someone else. You can't write something that will move other people if you haven't been moved yourself. Your only way to yourself is through your own voice. Your only way to writing with power is through your own voice.

What if your voice is no good, boring, uninteresting, unexotic? That's a fear we all have. But once you are willing to trust your own voice, you begin to find that the more you write the more comfortable you are. The more comfortable you are the more you get down on paper. Parts of yourself start appearing on the paper, and they are like a mirror—you discover you *do* have things to say, things that are powerful in their own right. This is one of the most important functions of freewriting. By writing without judgment, without trying to sound *correct* or like a writer, you begin to get your own voice on paper.

When you are talking to someone your voice comes through very clearly. You generally have a specific attitude toward your listener and a message you want to get across. Look at this list and think of a person you want to address in each category.

1. Someone you want praise from, or someone you want to praise.

   _____

2. Someone you're furious at.

   _____

3. Someone you're disgusted by.

   _____

4. Someone you feel sorry for.

   _____

5. Someone you want to warn or protect.

   _____

6. Someone you love who doesn't know of your love.

_____

7. Someone who is gone because of death or circumstance, but to whom you would still like to say goodbye.

_____

8. Someone you want to say something to but know you'd better not.

_____

Look at the people you have listed. Which of them would you like to have as your subject now? Whom would you like to speak to now? Circle your subject.

Exercise

For ten minutes direct your freewriting to addressing this person, telling her or him what's on your mind. Since she or he will never read what you write unless you choose to show it, say just what you want to say, in whatever way you want to say it. If you feel bitter write with bitterness; if you feel generous write with generosity. Do not let the editor stop you or force you to be reasonable or sensible. If the editor tries to stop you write down what she or he says. You are writing to hear clearly your own voice in this situation.

Write steadily and do not rush.

WANDERING TO FIND A SUBJECT

Wander through your memories. Wandering is the method we're exploring here, so take some time to wander and look. Enjoy yourself. You can do this on paper or in your mind, whatever seems to help you the most.

Look at images, recalling not only entire events but single pictures, moments —the small, seemingly inconsequential memories that stick with you, as well as the more striking ones. See what memories are triggered by the words here; some may trigger more memories than others. Let the memories themselves trigger other memories.

Think back to yesterday and find a memory. Can you find one from ten years ago? When you were twenty? Ten? Eight? Six? Three?

Does the month July send up a memory? September? A particular time of day? Sunset, for example? Midnight?

Does the color green trigger a memory? Aqua? Pink or rose? The smell of hyacinths, honeysuckle, garbage, liver?

Does the word *dance* give you a picture? Do you see something in the word *under*? *Dream*? *Laugh*? *Kiss*? *Tickle*? Let your mind supply more details until you can see the picture or event clearly.

Keep wandering until a memory you'd like to spend more time with stands out. If several memories want your attention, choose any one. You can go back to another one later.

Look more carefully at this memory.

Where are you? What kind of light is there? What do you notice? Are there any particular colors?

What do you hear clearly? In your mind? In the distance? Do you hear certain machines? Animals? Conversations?

Do you notice a certain smell? Is there an odor or fragrance connected with this memory?

Do you touch specific surfaces? What tastes are associated with this time?

What are you doing? How are you moving? Is there a particular sensation in your body?

Are there other people around? Are they moving in particular ways? Do they have a relationship to you?

Do certain thoughts occur to you? Certain questions?

Is this memory dark or light? Fast or slow? Hazy or distinct?

Exercise

Stay with this memory as long as you like. When you begin to write, forget all these questions. Forget the picture you've created in your mind. Try to write your memory as if you were seeing it for the first time; that way you won't feel obligated to reconstruct or fill in exactly what you have remembered. Make sure your memory starts in a specific place and is focused.

Write steadily, but do not rush. Acknowledge distractions, make comments, ask questions when necessary.

CLICHÉ

Put down the first word that comes to mind. Do not try to be creative.

white as _____

fat as _____

soft as _____

sharp as _____

light as _____

thin as _____

cold as _____

hard as _____

mad as _____

A cliché is an expression that is trite or hackneyed, worn out from overwork, used so often that it lacks freshness and originality. A cliché is an expression we have heard so often that *we do not have to think to retrieve it:* $1+1=2$; $2+2=4$; smooth as silk; $4+4=8$; green as grass. When we use a cliché people nod before we finish the phrase. It's like a quiz: It was cold as...(nod, nod) ...my feet when I walk in the snow in boots that leak. (What? Not ice? I thought you were going to say "cold as ice.")

When we use a cliché we don't have to think about the words we're saying. When we hear a cliché we don't have to listen; we know what's going to come next. Clichés are like our neighborhoods or the roads we take to work every day. They have become so familiar that we don't have to pay attention. We know what's there...or do we?

Occasionally you may *experience* a cliché. If, for example, you find a feather and lift it and are honestly astonished at how light it is, the phrase "light as a feather" may pop into your mind. "That's right," you may say. "Nothing could be lighter than this feather. "

It is the personal discovery of what *light* means, or *cold* or *black* or *smooth*, that provides the key to escaping cliché. Once in a while we may rediscover clichés personally, but they are still difficult to use in writing. We have no guarantee that our readers will rediscover along with us, and every expectation that they will dismiss the clichés we use as just that. So, for our own sake and that of our readers, it's usually best to explore and go beyond the expected if we want our words to evoke a certain feeling.

55

CLICHÉ

Directed Freewriting
Kay Levinson

> Green as grass. That's what people always say and sometimes it's true that on a clear blue day nothing is as green as green grass (how much grass is really green like that?) and on a winter day a yard of zoysia is the only color and then that *is* green. But now I think of eyes. I notice people with green eyes; the greenness attracts me. Maybe because it makes a person's eyes look mysterious. It makes me feel as if there's another world behind their eyes. Back to green though. Let me look in my mind and around me and see green things—green as an apple. Green as this wastebasket, as moldy cheese, the trees outside the science building, L's coat. My thoughts keep going back to the green eyes; that is a green that sets off a feeling in me. That is GREEN to me, the magic of green.

Exercise

Try to discover what some common words mean to you. What is *smooth* to you? What is the smoothest thing you know? The thing that makes you really understand smoothness? The thing by which you judge all smoothness? What about *black*?

Do not try to figure things out in your mind first. Use directed freewriting to hunt out the meaning. You may begin with a cliché and then keep freewriting/brainstorming, jumping from image to image until you arrive at the comparison that *is* the meaning to you. Imagine that your fingers are really touching particular smooth things, that you are seeing things that are black. This may help you generate material.

For ten minutes direct your freewriting to this exercise. You may spend the whole time on one word, or you may want to try several of the words below. You may find yourself asking questions, commenting, digressing. You may hit comparisons that aren't right at all. Don't worry. That's part of the gathering process. Keep going until you find the comparison that feels right to you.

1. smooth as . . .
2. black as . . .
3. hot as . . .
4. fast as . . .
5. dry as . . .
6. straight as . . .
7. green as . . .

INTRODUCING COMPARISON

What Is a Simile?
What Is a Comparison?

Both simile and metaphor express comparison. A simile uses the words *like* or *as*. A metaphor does not.

In the following list put an *M* by each sentence that contains a metaphor and an *S* by each sentence that uses a simile. Underline the two things that are being compared.

   __M__ That <u>paper</u> is <u>razor</u> sharp.
   __S__ That <u>paper</u> is as sharp as a <u>razor</u>.
   _____ My friend brought me a pool that felt like the beach.
   _____ Locker, my sincere friend, you are like a garbage compactor.
   _____ Your skin is made of pure cotton.
   _____ My cat, you are as black as the night rising new.
   _____ The butterfly's wings are paper-thin.
   _____ Your stomach is a pillow.

What Do Similes and Metaphors Do?

Simile and metaphor are not decorations used to make a sentence sound better or more interesting. Simile and metaphor are tools with which to communicate precise observations: That paper is not merely sharp; it is a precise kind of sharp, like a razor!

But it is the nature of comparison to do more than point out a precise fact. For comparison is based on using the qualities of something familiar to explain something that is not familiar, and in the process of doing this we get more than facts.

My Sweater
Sari Elkins

It had worms for buttons
and strings black as the day I cut myself
and had to go to the hospital.

Does Sari like her sweater? Would she be saying the same thing if she stated the facts — that the sweater has black strings and ugly buttons?

Sari would be describing her sweater if she related those facts, but what she writes says more. She compares buttons we've never seen to worms. She compares the color of strings we've never seen to the day she cut herself. And suddenly we see these strings and buttons. Usually nondescript objects, they now take on the ugliness and terror of worms and accidents.

When I Write
Olga Marrero

When I write I feel like a new Olga.
I think I'm in a new galaxy
where no one lives and it's really quiet.

Does Olga like to write? Would she be saying the same thing if she said, "I get quiet when I write"? Or are we given a whole new dimension when Olga compares the expansive feeling of writing to a new galaxy, a huge space? Since we can never really go inside her mind, she finds a way to let us enter her feeling; she quiets us in her uninhabited galaxy.

For each comparison write one sentence that tells the objective fact conveyed by that comparison.

> Walt, you are a box of jokes that makes me laugh as much as if I and a friend had a lot of gum in our mouths so when we tried to talk it turned our words into sounds that were very funny.—*David Adelson*

_____

> Liver, your smell is like a bloody battlefield.

_____

> She puts on makeup like she is an eggshell.

_____

> The wood of my shotgun feels like a tree without the bark on it.

_____

Once you've practiced finding them, similes and metaphors can flow easily, but they're not always apt. Therefore, when you are using comparisons to describe an object or state, don't judge each one you write. Brainstorm as many as you can think of. Keep generating material. Then, when you are finished, go back and look them over to see which ones feel right.

Exercise

For ten minutes direct your freewriting to examining the outside of a fruit or vegetable, using comparison as a technique for discovery. Some of the qualities you might pay attention to include: color, texture, shape, smell, pattern, taste. Use whatever senses are activated by this fruit or vegetable.

You may write more slowly and spend more time on this exercise since you are looking and writing simultaneously. The danger is that you will begin to judge or plan what you write before you commit it to paper. Remember that you are still using the principles of freewriting: do not try to figure out a "good" comparison. Include ways you feel toward the object, questions, comments that occur to you. If you think of a comparison that doesn't seem to make sense, don't jump to conclusions. Write it down.

GOING OUT ALONE II

Do you feel like going out on your own? You now have many ways of finding a subject and writing about that subject.

1. Your subject may come from freewriting, beginning with a survey of your mind or of the concrete things around you.
2. You may already have a subject that interests you, and you can brainstorm to break it down or direct your freewriting to focus it.
3. You may want to spark a memory by thinking of the phrase "a time I . . ." or by wandering.
4. Whatever your subject, you can write in present or past tense, in first or third person. We haven't tried writing a memory in second person ("You walk up the steps"), but you may want to try it on your own.
5. You may want to be a camera and record yourself or someone else, at this moment or in a scene from the past.
6. You may have something to say to someone, something you can't say directly.
7. Maybe you want to look at an object by using comparison, talking to it or about it.

Whichever you choose (and it may not even be anything listed here), remember that the principles of freewriting—reserving judgment, getting everything onto the paper, and concentrating on concrete details—will help you connect with your energy and be active in your writing.

Of course, if all this talk makes you nervous, there's no rush. Go on to the next lesson.

Exercise

For ten minutes write steadily, without rushing, reserving judgment.

FINDING COMPARISONS

Associating comes naturally to everyone. We come to know an object or feeling in part by noticing how it is more like one thing than like another. When I look at the lines in my hand, I see that they are like a map, not like a picket fence. This process of linkage helps us make sense of the flood of new information we receive every day. It invests one piece of information with the qualities and power of another. My perception of the lines of my hand becomes enriched by the qualities I associate with a map—the sense of terrain, maybe, or the idea of routes going somewhere. Often such images just pop into our heads, making us conscious of the connections being made all the time in our minds. Sometimes crazy images pop up. We get the sudden, intense feeling that a person is like a sheet of steel. Where did that come from? we might wonder, and yet it feels right. Writers draw freely on this faculty of comparison, using it to discover new qualities, new feelings, new meanings in what they are writing about. They use comparison to make a description more precise or more powerful.

We want to keep in touch with the place where the mind discovers connections, but sometimes the road to that place gets clogged or keeps making the same tired detours ("red as a rose," "cold as ice"). How can we explore further, take a different route, get unstuck?

One way to make comparisons is to be aware of the parts of an object and their characteristics. Here is my hand, but my hand is made up of many parts: nails, knuckles, fingers. Any of them can spark an association: my spread fingers look like a fan, my curled finger looks like a baby sleeping. I didn't think of these similarities right away. They didn't pop into my mind. But by analyzing the parts of the object I'm describing and by then looking carefully at them, I can call up comparisons that are revealing and powerful.

Let's say you've looked hard at the parts of your hand but still nothing comes up. You're looking at your hand, and it just looks like a hand to you no matter how hard you try to see it differently. Try comparing your hand to *anything*. Don't wait to see whether the comparison works. Just arbitrarily and irresponsibly connect two things that have no business being connected. Pull a word from the dictionary. Look around the room. Grab the first word that comes into your mind. (My hand is like a rocketship. My hand is like a turtle.) Now explore these connections. Some of them will seem silly. Others may seem to make a little sense, and a few may be surprisingly appropriate, may even get you to discover your hand in some new way.

When we are writing, these methods of finding comparisons get all jumbled up. We jump from one method to the other, trying to keep the road open. The advantage of being aware of them is that when we run dry in one direction, we have another way to go. When we want to surprise ourselves, we have ways to go about it.

FINDING COMPARISONS

Exercise

For two or three minutes look at your hand and list its parts. (fingers, veins, webs). Also list parts of parts (the parts of your fingers, etc.).

For ten minutes direct your freewriting to looking at your hand and making comparisons. Remember that if your associations stop coming naturally you can look at the parts of your hand to trigger comparisons. If that goes dead you can try arbitrarily forcing comparisons.

Reserve judgment and get onto paper whatever comes into your mind, including distractions. The freewriting will keep your mind limber and help it leap to images you may not expect.

EXTENDING IMAGES

Directed Freewriting
Mary Ellen Bosch

Hand, when you clench you look like a hermit crab that protects some small helpless thing from being seen. When you open and close you look like a neon sign blinking on and off, shouting an urgent message to look and join in. It surprises me to think that you are so gentle and so demanding at the same time. I would like to be the crab or the turtle protected by you. You would make me feel warm. I would invite my friends to come inside you. You would open your thumb wide and we would enter. It would be a party.

But when you are a neon sign I do not want to be near you. You hurt my eyes like red furniture does. You insist that I look and act as if I didn't get your message the first time and you say it over and over and I ask you to stop. You could be doing other things. You don't need to blink on and off. So I unplug you and you unstretch and lie limp and I try to find out what you were trying to say when you were flashing on and off.

Do you like to be different things at different times? Do you like to demand attention? Do you like people to cuddle or recoil from you?

Read the following sentences carefully. Note your reaction to them and visualize the pictures they suggest.

My opening and closing hand looks like a neon sign.
My outstretched hand looks like the wing of a bird.
My clenched fist looks like a prehistoric lizard.

Now read the following and do the same.

My opening and closing hand is like a neon sign blinking on and off, shouting an urgent message to look and join in.
My outstretched hand is like the wing of a soaring bird when it has caught a supporting wind.
My clenched fist is like a prehistoric lizard hunched up against the cold.

When we look at an object as if it is the thing we have compared it to, as if the hand *is* the neon sign, *is* the bird, *is* the lizard, we can extend the image so that it becomes more precise and more visual.

If we describe our wiggling fingers as a spider, we are obviously not talking about a spider sitting in its web or feeding on its prey. We are *probably* describing a spider crawling up a wall or dangling in midair. But which? By looking closely at our fingers and deciding exactly what they are doing, we are compelling the specific image, the exact picture, to come alive and make us feel its power, its rightness.

The key words, either implied or stated, in extending an image are *that* and *when:*

It looks like a bird *that is* . . .
It looks like a bird *when the bird is* . . .

Stretch your fingers out and back as far as they can go. When I do that, my fingers remind me of an ocean wave. What do your fingers remind you of when they stretch out and back like that?

_____

_____

When my fingers stretch back and look like a wave and I look again, it seems to me that this particular wave has just reached its crest and is about to break. Extend your simile as I extended mine (now my fingers are not like any wave but like one that is cresting and about to break). See your simile more clearly so that it is precise and gives an exact picture, a specific image.

When my fingers stretch they look like _____

that/when _____

Wiggle your fingers. Watch them. What do your fingers remind you of when they wiggle like that?

_____

Look at your fingers as if they are that thing. Extend your simile so it is more precise, more vivid.

_____

_____

Snap your fingers. What do your fingers remind you of when they snap?

_____

Look at and listen to your fingers as they snap. Extend the image so it is more precise and more vivid.

_____

_____

Exercise

Brainstorm ways your hand can move.

_____   _____   _____

_____   _____   _____

_____   _____   _____

For ten minutes direct your freewriting to exploring, through comparison, one or more ways in which your hand moves. Look hard at your hand moving. Extend the images so they are precise and vivid. Do not be cautious with your similes and extensions. Whether they pop into your mind, come from analysis, or are forced, let them go on the paper.

You may spend your whole time extending a single simile, or you may jump from one to another.

TALKING ABOUT THE INTANGIBLE

How can you describe your state of mind when you can't think? Or the sensation inside your body when you feel out of control? Or the feeling of seeing something breathtaking, the feeling of being exhilarated?

These are feelings, sensations, that cannot be described in concrete terms. They are responses to concrete situations but are themselves intangible. Simile and metaphor provide a way to talk concretely about such feelings or states of mind, both to see them more clearly ourselves and to share them.

Entering the Image

Sometimes an image moves us to such an extent that we find ourselves wanting to go inside it, to tell more and more about it until it is real.

> When I am looking for an idea I feel as though I am searching to get through to something but I can't get by the fence. —*Judy Danish*

Once we are inside, we can either stay there and explore or find ways of changing the reality.

Directed Freewriting
Judy Danish

> I'm searching to get through to something but I can't get by the fence. The links appear to be an impenetrable mesh but they are really a semi-permeable membrane. I can feel the larva of ideas coming through the fence to me but the butterfly can't become until it can get through the fence. My hiking boots jab into footholds as I climb but I still can't reach over the top. Back on the ground I scramble back and forth but there is no end to the fence. I collapse, just fold up. And there's the break in the mesh. It's small but as I scratch and claw it gapes and I finally get through.

If we break this process down we find that it often has the following structure: finding a simile, extending the simile until it is real, entering that reality.

What does your mind feel like when you can't think?
When I can't think I feel a brick wall in my mind.

Can you tell us more about that brick wall?
It's that sick pink brick, and it's to the top of my brain, and so I'm trapped in a small corner.

What can you do so you will be able to think?
I push on every brick and finally find a loose one. I push it out, rip out the next and the next, one by one. The more I push the easier it gets, until the whole wall crumbles.

What does your mind feel like when you have a lot of ideas at once?

Can you say more about it? Extend your image so it becomes real and you can enter it.

_____

_____

_____

Now that you are inside it, what do you want to do?

_____

_____

_____

Choose one of these states of mind or another one that interests you to use as your subject for this lesson:

1. Feeling out of control
2. Not being able to think
3. Being confused
4. Getting an idea
5. Feeling sleepy
6. Feeling content
7. Feeling sad
8. Feeling excited

Exercise

For ten minutes direct your freewriting to describing that feeling by comparison. When you find a comparison that feels right, tell more about it; extend it until it becomes real and you can enter it. Once there, you may want to see what happens or try to change the situation or maintain the state. React to it as if it were definitely real. Allow yourself the freedom to put on paper whatever you see happening. Go with diversions and distractions when necessary.

Remember, you are describing an inner state, not what you do, but what you feel, what no one else can see. Get your details by paying attention to that feeling, as if you had it now.

A CASE FOR BEAUTY

There are many tangible, measurable ways to evaluate something you've read. Maybe you want to find out what happens next; the writing has hooked you. That's one good way. Maybe what the writer is presenting feels true to you. That's another way. You may read a piece that's concrete, full of details; you can see it happening right on the page. Terrific! But what do you make of the criterion that it's aesthetically satisfying, it's beautiful?

Beauty, in a piece of writing, doesn't have to mean a pretty image or a pretty subject. It's much larger than that. The aesthetic criterion accounts for the little gasp we feel as writers when we've managed to create something living on the page: a fresh insight, a polished image, a certain juxtaposition of one phrase with another, the particular rhythm of the words and sound of the letters. These are some of the pleasures of writing that are not easily explained.

Kelly Sayers

> The wind is strong
> The weed is gone
> sh sh sh

Now is a time for sitting still, letting the experience of those words ripple larger and larger in us, allowing ourselves to feel moved.

It helps to limit the scope of a piece of writing to a single natural image so we can really feel how it moves us, how it moves inside us.

Edward Turner

> A piece of grass.
> Soft. Green. Slippery grass
> changing its shape.

The precision of these lines can suggest a whole season, while this—

Anonymous

> Winter. I love it.
> Then the weather is cold
> and everyone's happy.

—has no evocative power at all. One image is alive; one is dead. As writers, we have to be willing to feel deeply if we want to get feeling into our writing. We have to read and see with a willingness, a desire, to be moved.

The observer sees something and is struck by it and tries to put it into the image:

Jeanette Diaz

> Trees branching out—
> the leaves trying
> to get their air.

or hears something:

José Acevedo

> The rain splashes
> on the window.
> Click! Another pebble.

or sees the likeness of one thing to another:

A CASE FOR BEAUTY

José Acevedo

> A tree—big muscles
> like the strongest man in the world.
> A model pose.

or sees a juxtaposition of color:

Ceddrick Whitehead

> A big black pole
> with roses around it.
> Pop! Another rose.

and struggles to recreate the surprise and pleasure of that simple discovery.

Exercise

For ten or more minutes direct your attention to everything natural around you: plants, water, animals, sky, rain, snow, the elements! Go outside if you need more room. Walk around with paper and pen and get down image after image (the image is the single picture that suddenly strikes you). No long sentences full of adjectives and adverbs describing what you see. No big themes. You are looking for a single image, a precise movement, a sound, a simile, a particular light, a juxtaposition of color or shape or size.

When you're through collecting, take your images and sit quietly with them. Work with the ones you like best. Get the verb just right and the sound just right and the simile just right. Pare each down to three short lines, to a single image. Find the ones that move you when you read them, that make your chest feel a shift in it.

FINDING SOMETHING IN NOTHING

Looking at N.
Kay Levinson

N. Eating
When she swallows
she leaves a crumb behind on her lips.
I wipe my mouth
to give her a hint,
but she just keeps talking.

N. Playing Tennis
Like a spring, a frog, a panther, a yo-yo
She pops, she crouches, she leaps, she retracts.

N. Getting Mad
She rocks back and forth
until she's swallowed her anger.
It blooms into a terrible silence
with invisible thorns.

When it seems nothing is going on and we have nothing to write, there is often an untapped wealth of detail. At the least this detail yields a picture of what we have observed. It may go so far as to reveal a truth or an attitude that we hadn't detected or that we'd noticed but hadn't really absorbed.

We are going to use *snapshots* to find this something in nothing. Snapshots combine our skills in being a camera and making precise observations with our skills in charging the language with similes, metaphors, verbs, sensory details. Reread the above snapshots and notice the techniques the writer has used.

As opposed to a *movie*, which tells a sequential story, or a *panorama*, which gives a broad view or general impression, a *snapshot* is a sharply focused picture of an ordinary action: someone talking on the telephone, looking in the mirror, peeling an orange, tying a shoe.

Write the names of some people you know.

_____   _____   _____

_____   _____   _____

_____   _____   _____

Star the person you'd like to have as your subject for these snapshots.

Brainstorm activities you've observed this person engaging in. For example, being cranky, getting dressed, playing a specific game or a specific instrument. Follow the person visually in your mind so you can get a range of their activities.

_____   _____   _____

_____ _____ _____

_____ _____ _____

_____ _____ _____

Spend a few minutes with this list, seeing your subject engaged in these activities.

Exercise

For ten minutes direct your freewriting to writing snapshots. Choose one activity to record in your first snapshot. Remember, you are not telling a story ("Once D. was brushing his teeth and . . ."). You are showing a simple action using the devices you have been practicing: verbs, similes, sensory detail.

Try at least three activities. Your writing may go a little more slowly, but you are still sticking faithfully to the principle of not editing, of putting on paper what comes to your mind. You may want to show each action in a separate section, like the N. snapshots, rather than writing a solid paragraph. This will make you more aware of each word.

Fantasy can be dangerous in writing. It is so easy to turn out an imitation fantasy, an imitation tall tale, an imitation superstory. Such products may sound similar to the original, but they're just a superficial filling-in of formulas. If you read one, they're all easy to copy: have a princess saddled with a cruel stepmother; have a superhero saving someone with a laser beam.

But the whole point of this book has been to get you away from imitation so you learn and trust that you have something to say. I've been steering you away from fantasy and invented plots on the ground that it is better to stick to what you know while you search out your own voice.

Now that you're able to use facts instead of generalizations, now that you're used to writing in your own voice, now that you realize you do have experiences and feelings to write about, you are ready for the fun of escaping the constraints of the literal truth. You are ready to try writing fantasy from your new perspective.

What makes a fantasy more than an imitation of a style? For one thing, it is told *as if* it were real. You don't stop using details just because you're writing fantasy. In fact, if you expect your reader, or yourself, to take a leap of faith and believe the preposterous, you're going to *have* to use convincing detail. For another thing, fantasy does not have to be lightweight. It is anything imagined. It can be somber, quiet, funny, silly, eerie, outrageous.

Start your fantasy by grounding yourself in the concrete detail. List some things you've done today, things that happen every day; for example, "I listened to music," "I looked out my window," "I was reprimanded."

_____	_____	_____
_____	_____	_____
_____	_____	_____
_____	_____	

One way to make a fantasy is to exaggerate — to stretch the truth until it is a huge, wonderful lie.

Directed Freewriting
Katherine Baer

> You yelled at me today. I told you not to but you kept on, so I jumped up from the chair screaming as if I was murdered. I threatened you with my fist and saw you afraid, then told you in a low, mean voice your faults, how you mispronounce words, how you keep talking when everyone is bored, how you assume people care what you think. I continued to talk, talk, talk until you were crying and sorry and disappeared.

Another way to make a fantasy is to turn the expected into the unexpected.

Directed Freewriting
Mary Ellen Bosch

It was quiet in my house. I was alone. I decided that I wanted to listen to some music. I put on some classical station and lay down on my bed. As I listened I heard a click in the radio. I looked and was happy to find that this music was entering my home. It was coming out in round notes and quarter notes and whole notes and quick eighths and sixteenths, holding hands and laughing. They looked like all kinds of people happy to be doing what they were doing, glad to be together and enjoying each other. They came and sat on my chairs and floors and pillows. Some even sat on the plaster wall bumps. The lighter ones floated in the air. The deeper tones sat more formally. Without saying a word they all seemed to be involved in a great buzz session. Some sat on my bed and confided in me. They knew I felt happy to be with them and I saw my blanket floating like a magic carpet. I travelled with this music for a long time, it seemed.

Take several of the everyday occurrences you listed and try exaggerating. For example:

You yelled at me today and I got angry. I wanted to jump up screaming as if I was being murdered.

When I looked out the window I saw the old lady in white boots walking her little dog. I wanted to turn into a camera and watch her in all the private parts of her life.

_____

_____

_____

_____

Take several of the things you do every day and turn the expected into the unexpected. For example:

I listened to music. Instead of just hearing it I could see it in the room.

I washed my face. Instead of seeing it get cleaner I found I had scrubbed off my old face and a new one appeared.

_____

_____

_____

_____

_____

Exercise

Look back at the sentences you just wrote exaggerating your response to something or turning the expected into the unexpected. Which interests you as a subject? Or do they trigger another idea you would prefer to write about?

For ten minutes direct your freewriting to building a fantasy on this subject. Don't feel you have to stick to the truth. Let your writing lead you. It may take you in a direction that is crazy, tragic, hilarious, or quiet. Remember, the more detailed and visual your writing, the more believable it will be, no matter how wild the story is.

Write steadily, but do not rush.

GOING OUT ALONE III

You may want to take this chance to go out alone and see what you know. You have many ways now of finding a subject and writing about it. You can:

1. freewrite a mirror of your mind;
2. direct your freewriting by *trying on* various concrete things around you — objects, smells, textures — letting them lead you to a subject or begin a series of thoughts;
3. describe the place you are in now, paying attention to the concrete, sensory details, or put yourself in another place you feel positively or negatively about and look at that place through writing;
4. direct your freewriting to exploring a subject or problem that is on your mind;
5. explore a particular memory you find by wandering or by thinking of specific times or specific verbs and letting them trigger memories;
6. observe yourself or someone else in the past or present or future as precisely and objectively as if you were a camera, in a long shot or in snapshots;
7. address someone you feel strongly about in the privacy of your writing and in the voice that captures your attitudes toward them;
8. look carefully at an object and your feelings toward that object by using comparison, extending your comparisons so they are precise;
9. examine a way you are feeling now by using comparison to describe it and then entering that comparison and even changing that intangible state;
10. search for beauty — for the small image, the sound or texture or juxtaposition that moves you — and then fine-tune the phrases you have collected;
11. escape the literal truth by exaggerating your response to something or turning the expected into the unexpected, never forgetting the details;
12. make new combinations using any of these approaches.

Exercise

Whatever you choose (and it may not even be anything listed here), remember that the principles of freewriting — writing steadily, neither rushing nor crawling; reserving judgment; getting everything on the paper — will help you connect with your energy and be active in your writing. And directing your freewriting — getting more and more focused and seeing the concrete sensory detail — will make your writing more powerful so that it moves both you and your readers.

WRITING

Well, it's almost time for us to part. I've learned a tremendous amount writing this book, and I hope you've had the same experience working in it. If you've been writing steadily, trying to get past your misconceptions, being honest to your feelings and observations, you're beginning to be able to use the language of writing. You understand some of the assumptions of writing. You can find a subject and gather details. You can get words on paper. You have ways to charge the language: sensory details and verbs and metaphor and voice and exaggeration and other techniques you may have stumbled across yourself as you wrote. Perhaps you've even begun to take responsibility for your writing, going out alone and facing the blank page yourself. Quite an accomplishment! Of course there are still problems — all of the above, for example — but they are problems all writers wrestle with constantly.

When you first started this book you directed your freewriting to exploring your feelings and experiences as a writer. Now that you are at the end of the beginning, I think you'll find it worthwhile to spend this time looking back at what you have written, rereading your first directed freewriting, and then directing this freewriting to thinking again about you and writing. I wouldn't presume to suggest how you do that, or even how much time to take — you're in charge now!

Exercise

INTO THE CLASSROOM

INTRODUCTION

Now that you have begun to understand writing from the point of view of a writer, I want to give you some concrete suggestions about how to take this sensibility into your classroom. I want to suggest the kinds of questions you can ask to help students find a subject or make their writing more detailed; I want to offer ways to respond to what they write and ways to avoid having to grade everything they write. All these techniques are based on the writing experience you have just had, so you will be in familiar territory hearing familiar language. If you feel shaky about your writing, don't worry. If you're not madly in love with writing, that's okay. You probably see writing from a slightly different point of view now. You understand some of the key elements that make writing stronger, you are aware of the problems a writer may encounter, and you know the importance of separating the editor from the writer; and because of these insights you'll probably find that there's a change both in you and in your students when you bring writing into your classroom.

You may feel awkward at first. Don't let that stop you. Watch yourself and your students to see what works and what doesn't. Let your students help you. Don't forget that they need exactly what adults need: a safe place to experiment, a lot of time to practice, freedom from constant correction, and encouragement and ideas to help them delve further into this sometimes difficult language. With writing as with any other skill, you will become more comfortable as you continue to teach it. And as you help your students, you will be sharpening your own writing skills. At some point you will be surprised to find that what once may have seemed foreign is now familiar and that writing has become an important and natural part of your school day.

THE TEACHER AS AUTHORITY

When I ask my students to write about what is important to them, I am requiring of them a great deal of courage—courage to explore their most personal thoughts and feelings, and courage to subject those explorations to public scrutiny. If I am going to ask so much of them, I must be willing to give them the freedom from criticism they need to have that courage. I must recognize that if I establish myself as an absolute authority on what is good writing and what is not, on what is permissible and what is not, I automatically condition what a student will write.

There are many points during the writing lesson where I ask myself questions to be sure that I am listening to what the students are trying to tell me and that I am allowing them the freedom from judgment and censorship they need to acquire the courage to express themselves.

Do the students understand the lesson?

The more precisely my students understand what I am trying to teach, the more focused and powerful their writing becomes. I encourage them to question what I say; I listen to their responses, I look at the expressions on their faces, I gauge the extent of their interest. If I have to generate more examples, approach the lesson from another angle, or rephrase a question, I am not hesitant to do so.

Am I going for a specific answer?

Our assumptions are communicated in our tone of voice and the words we choose. Sometimes I catch myself expecting or waiting for one particular insight: for example, "Wiggling fingers look like a spider." Students may offer other interesting images for how fingers look when they wiggle, but I don't focus on their responses. I cut short ideas, listening for the one I have in mind. Gradually, students pick up on this and start trying to guess the "right answer," further limiting their range of ideas and the excitement I want to encourage in the classroom. If I am going to keep the circuits open to that current of excitement, I must listen to myself to be sure I am not giving subtle messages about what I want to hear.

Am I listening/reading as a censor or judge?

One of the most difficult conflicts between teacher and student can occur when the teacher feels uncomfortable with the student's subject or attitude toward the subject.

The Fight with the Bad Question
Danny Batanian, 3

Once I was doing my work in school and a dirty question came to me. Then I said, "Ay, you, you, do you want to go away or do you want to fight? If I write about you the teacher will get mad."

He said, "Well, I better fight." Then he punched me in the face and I punched him in the face.

And then the teacher came in and said, "What are you doing Danny? Are you crazy, fighting with yourself?"

I said, "I was fighting with the bad question."

She said, "Get out of this room." And that was the end of me.

As a writer I believe that every part of our experience should be available as a subject for our writing, that this freedom is what allows a person to develop into a strong, confident, and honest writer.

Freedom sometimes encourages students to take on difficult attitudes or experiences in their writing. When these not-so-pleasant subjects arise, they cannot be made to vanish by simply ignoring them or encouraging students to choose another topic. If students sense my discomfort with a subject or see me as a censor, it is likely that they will shy away from provocative material or stop writing honestly altogether.

When it comes to publishing a piece of writing, I use stricter standards. At that stage it is sometimes necessary to change words or names, and some pieces may not be appropriate for publication at all. Students will usually feel these distinctions themselves. However, considerations of what is appropriate have no place at the writing stage; they are editorial concerns.

Therefore, in a situation where a student has written something that makes me uncomfortable or angry, I try to deal with it as a writer: that is, instead of making a judgment on the material, I may comment on the quality of the writing, on the success or failure of the writer to see details or bring the scene to life on the page. Sometimes I ask the student to consider the situation from another point of view. For example, if Jim writes a piece condoning stealing, I might ask if he has ever had something stolen from him or ask him to imagine that he is the owner of the stolen bike. But I must be careful not to become too moralistic or expect the student to rewrite the piece according to my framework of values.

When students use obscenities I try to determine whether they are testing me to see if I really allow the freedom I profess or whether the swear words were actually used during the incident being described. In the first case I don't comment on the obscenities, and there is usually no further testing. In the second case I permit the obscenities. If their work is to be published the students themselves will almost always want to change obscenities to make it more acceptable. If they don't want to and I feel that the publication of such words could cause more trouble than their importance to the story justifies, I exercise my editorial authority.

The freedom I give students sometimes unleashes writing about taboo subjects such as sex or bathroom incidents. Again, once students have tested my willingness to let them say what's on their minds, these subjects begin to lose their illicit glamor. I have found that this writing occurs less often as I become more skilled in helping students find their source of energy.

Student writing about volatile, off-limits subjects like sex and drugs can be dangerous for both teacher and student. If a student asks permission to write about such an experience, I generally grant it. I acknowledge the possible danger and request that I be the sole reader of the piece. This arrangement has never caused me or, as far as I know, my students any problems. Of course, its privacy must be honored by the teacher as well as by the student.

Occasionally a student shows such an attitude of violence or prejudice towards an individual or group that I feel compelled to criticize the piece, not as a writer, but as a person with particular values. Before I talk to the student I try to make this distinction very clear so that neither of us will confuse my role and the student will not feel that all future writing efforts will be judged.

Do I really want to know?

If I am not really interested in what students are saying, they will feel it. I always try to listen, not because I am supposed to, but because I want to know what happened and because I want to give students the energy that comes from being listened to.

Am I asking too many questions?

When a student sighs or growls or mutters and stops talking, it's possible that I've pushed too hard, asked too many questions, made my questions more important than the student's story. The balancing act between teacher and student is delicate enough to need fine tuning and plenty of practice.

Do I appreciate the danger of writing?

Do you remember feeling hesitant to share, or even to write for yourself, some of your most personal feelings and experiences? When I ask students to reveal themselves in their writing, I must take seriously the vulnerability they are likely to feel. I must listen to myself to be sure that I don't abuse their feelings, that I don't belittle the experiences they are willing to share with me, that I don't cut them off in mid-story or dismiss their courage. I want them to feel safe and strong in their vulnerability so that they can put that strength into their writing. One protection I offer hesitant students who are grappling with sensitive memories or thoughts is the right to put an X at the top of their papers. This mark indicates that they want no one but me to read their work, or in some cases, where they so stipulate, not even me. I honor both requests.

Do I want the students to write my piece?

When I hear myself giving too many suggestions to a student — "Why don't you start here?" or "I have a great ending for you" or "Here's just the word you need" — I begin to get suspicious of myself. It doesn't matter if I think my idea would be better or would make more sense than what the student has written. I have to ask myself: Is this what Debbie *wants* to write? Is this *her* story? A young writer needs to learn how to make choices, just as I did when I started writing. It is easy, when your teacher makes a suggestion, to feel obliged to accept it or relieved that your problem is solved. My job in the writing class is to help students find out where they want to take their writing or which ending they like better, even if I would have chosen something different.

This doesn't mean, of course, that you can *never* make suggestions or show students that there is a strong case for a particular word or phrase. Just remember, it's *their* piece of writing, and they should be encouraged to make the final decision.

Do I give students credit for knowing themselves better than I know them?

If I give a lesson and my students aren't interested, should I insist that they follow along, or am I willing to see that they have distractions, concerns they need to go with? Remember how much time we spent in the workbook on acknowledging distractions? Children have distractions, too. I will have more success at stimulating students to write if I am also able to see their inability to write, their occasional listlessness or frustration. Let me give you two examples.

Charlie was sullen and was playing with a pencil when he was supposed to be writing about snow. I kept asking him questions to help him get a subject. He kept shaking his head, and then he started to cry. Finally I asked, "Is something wrong that you want to talk about?" He dictated the following poem:

People Shouldn't Curse in the Bathroom
Charlie Brown, 1

Nairobe was in the bathroom cursing.
Then I told him I was going to tell his teacher
And he told mine.
Now I am happy because I wrote this poem.

When he was finished, he went on to write about snow.

There have been times when a student's distraction became the subject of that day's writing. One day Antonio was feeling so sad that I suggested he write about his sadness:

Antonio Edwards, 1

Sad. Sad. Sad. Sad. Sad. Sad. Say
Say Dad. How come that
everything is sad?
But you know what?
One of these days
happy things are going to come up.
On Halloween.
Hey, Dad, these things are beginning
to get happy.
Barbara, everybody loves you.
I do too love you
and I wish that I would be able
to love and care for loving people.

Sometimes students so actively resist a subject that I have to give them credit for knowing that the subject may be dangerous to them. Sometimes students resist adding details so vehemently that I have to assume it isn't the time to push.

Am I listening to what is really in the writing?

Sometimes I make comments on a piece of writing during class, or even have a student make changes, only to realize later, while rereading the piece at my leisure, that I was wrong—the original writing was stronger without the changes I suggested. I've been sufficiently humbled over the years; now I try to read a piece carefully before I make suggestions.

Naturally I am not always successful in providing a completely safe and encouraging writing environment. But by watching myself, my responses to the students and their writing, I can become aware of my mistakes and try to change my behavior. This vigilance is necessary because listening and sharing authority are two dangerous, difficult, but vital features of the writing classroom.

THE TEACHER AS CRITIC

When students finish an assignment they bring their papers to me to find out if I like what they've written. This is a time of great anticipation for any writer — the first act of sharing. It requires a willingness on my part, as critic, to be *moved* by what I read, an attitude best accomplished by reading as a fellow writer rather than as an editor bent on detecting mechanical errors.

The greatest disservice a reader can do a piece of writing is to trivialize what, for the writer, is a sincere attempt at communicating. I have often heard adults say of a student's writing, "How cute" or "That's nice" or "Doesn't that *its* take an apostrophe?" If I want students to take pride in their writing, if I want to encourage them to push harder and take chances, I must read their work with a desire to be affected by it. I must try to point out places in the writing that have succeeded in moving me. And when I make suggestions I must direct them towards strengthening or clarifying the content of the piece rather than identifying its mechanical errors.

The following pages provide some specific guidelines for criticism.

Finding the invention, the word that works

Some teachers feel that if they always try to find something good in a piece of writing, they will end up lying to their students or encouraging a lazy, anything-goes attitude in the classroom. I find not only that it is easier than you might suspect to discover a well-chosen word or keen insight in most papers, but also that practicing this technique benefits both teacher and student. Looking for the strong parts sharpens my ability to listen and read, just as it takes the pressure off my students to write flawless first drafts. When I let them know that an entire piece of writing doesn't have to be strong in order for one part to be strong or even outstanding, I reinforce the idea that writing is a process, and one that takes a long time to perfect. When students know they have written one phrase or one sentence or one paragraph well, they are more likely to appreciate the weaknesses of other sections, and, confident that they can succeed at least in part, they are more willing to go back and tackle their problems in a piece.

Anonymous, 2

> One day I was angry because my mother screamed at me and she smack my face and I was getting angry and angry. When I am screaming my mother hate the noise. I am screaming tears from my mouth and now I am not angry no more and now I like my mother and father.

When you read this paragraph, did you feel distracted by the mechanical errors? Did they keep you from really reading the piece? Learn to distinguish between your editor's voice and your writer's voice when you read student writing. Reread the paragraph several times. What is happening? Do any changes occur in the story? In the language? Are there specific words or phrases that stand out to you?

The writer has adequately shown the progress and resolution of her anger, but what really jumps out at me is the phrase "I am screaming tears from my mouth." It is especially powerful because it forces me to visualize the violence of her anger. It forces the writer to react too; notice how at this point she changes from writing in past tense to writing in present tense, as if she were right there. If the whole piece was equally as strong it would probably lapse into melodrama, but as it stands the author has created a context for one powerful line. When I responded to the piece, I pointed this out to her and told her how much the image moved me. In trying to describe her anger she was forced to experiment with words, to create a way to say what she had felt. How did she discover such a sophisticated invention? I wonder. How did she know to switch tenses?

I am always looking for such inventions and pointing them out to the writer: a sound, a concrete detail, an observation, a metaphor, a repetition, or an invented word that the writer has forced out of herself in order to tell her story.

Finding the details that clarify

Sometimes students try to write stories but are unable to get the details on paper. Perhaps they remember that *something* happened, but they have not yet taken the time, or don't know how, to remember the details of the incident. Or perhaps they remember the incident clearly but can't distinguish between the full account in their minds and the sketchy account they have written down. My job is to help them recall the details and make sure they get those details on paper.

One day I got this story from a third grader:

> My auncl was drieving a car and he scrape five cars and he did not have no lens so he went to jale and I cry.

When you read this were you so distracted by the errors that you couldn't pay attention to the writing? Are there words you think you can't read? If so, go back and figure them out before you proceed. If a teacher has good intentions towards a piece of writing, few words will be illegible when they are read in context. Read this piece several times. Do you have an emotional response to the story? What does the story lack? How could you help the student?

There was no way I could respond to this piece of writing. The author's sadness didn't touch me at all. In order to respond to her experience I first had to help her fill in the scene with details. We had a dialogue that went something like this:

> *I'll bet you know more about this time than you've told us. Tell me, where were you when you saw this happening?*
> I was looking out the window because I couldn't go outside.
>
> *What happened when your uncle scraped the cars?*
> There was a man in the last car. He came out.
>
> *Do you remember anything about the way the man looked?*
> He had a frown.

Then what happened?

He punched my uncle in the face. I started laughing.

So, you did know more than you wrote down. Let me read you your story. Now we can see what happened more clearly.

While we were talking together I wrote down her responses, and they formed a new story.

Anonymous, 3

> I was looking out the window because I couldn't go outside. I saw my uncle driving a car and he scraped five cars. There was a man in the last car. He got out of his car. He had a frown. He punched my uncle in the face. I started laughing. But my uncle did not have a license so he went to jail and I cried.

The writing in this second version is still not great, but at least the story is starting to relate an event that the student and I can see. The part I like best is the vantage point of the writer, the way she is watching all of it from her window.

The Time I Was Scared Stiff
Hilton Worrell, Jr., 5

> One day in October my mother was haveing a baby (it's my little brother) we were going home and my mother and I stepped into the elevator. and when we reached the 11th and 12th floor the elevator stopped between two floors with such a jerk That my mother fell down. I was so scared i Just started Pressing all sorts of buttons. Then when I pressed the bell button the elevator went down and they took my mother to the hospital and she had the baby and it was a healthy boy!

Finding the emotional center

When you read this story were you distracted by the errors? Remember, we want students to focus their energy on the writing, so try to read past the errors to the content. The writer of this piece has included enough details so that we can see the event. What further details will make the piece stronger?

In responding to a short piece like this I aimed for details that would make the emotional center clearer. I was not interested in what Hilton and his mother were wearing or what kind of day it was. These *are* details, and in a longer piece they might set the event in context, but within the boundaries of this piece they won't really help us know what it was like *in that stuck elevator.* They won't let us feel the emotional center of the event.

What questions could I ask to get at the scared-stiff feeling of being trapped? I asked Hilton what thoughts went through his mind; if there was a window in the elevator and what he saw through it; if he heard noises outside the elevator. I asked what his mother did when she fell down. He replied that she sat in the corner, just crying. I asked what he did then. He said that at first he couldn't move at all and then he started pressing buttons, his arms swinging like crazy. I suggested that he add these details since they would help us see what was happening.

After spending time recalling details orally, a student will often go back and add only a fraction of those details. In this case, Hilton added the sentence "When she fell down I was so scared I did not move." Then he continued reading the piece to me, and when he came to "The elevator went down," he stopped and wrote in the word "slowly. " This is exactly what we are trying to work towards. It is this slow process—students coming to understand *for themselves* the importance of detail and learning to listen to their own words— that will make the biggest difference in their ability to write.

Life
Ava Garrison, 6

Life is sometimes wonderful with one too many a surprise.
Life is sometimes painful when someone dies.
Life is sometimes quick as we grow older by and by.
Life is sometimes joyful when there's only you and I.
Life is sometimes happy with the old man playing the fife.
But most of all and all of most, Life is just plain life.

Helping students change tracks

Notice that there are no mechanical errors in this piece.

Ava's poem is a good example of what can go wrong when the concrete details of experience are watered down to generalizations and the writer tries to adopt a "poetic voice." On first reading, things are not so bad: the rhyme isn't too forced; the writer has set up a structure of repetition; the generalizations aren't too farfetched. But read it several times. "One too many a surprise"? What does that mean, and what does it have to do with "wonderful"? "*Sometimes* painful when someone dies"? "The old man playing the fife"?

Undoubtedly people do generalize as they grow up and accumulate experiences, and certainly generalization has an important place in writing. The generalizations in "Life" may trigger memories or feelings in you, but if they do the writer can take little credit for having moved you. She is merely listing a series of "buzz words"—words like *joy* and *die*, which cannot help but elicit strong associations. Is this the point of writing—to make lists of potent, abstract words that could have been written by anyone and that provoke whatever memory or thought or feeling the reader chooses to supply?

No. A writer struggles to find the right words and the right point of view with which to convey a personal vision as clearly as possible. You may agree or disagree with this vision. You may come to a conclusion different from the writer's. But you do so on the basis of concrete evidence in the writing, and its author can take credit in the end for having produced an affecting piece.

I wanted to make this point clear to Ava, so I said to her, "You have written a poem here that tells us your view of life, but that view has come from specific experiences you've had. Can you pick one of these lines and show us a particular experience that made you come to see life in this way?" Ava came back fifteen minutes later with this:

Ava Garrison

> One night my cousin had to go to the hospital because there was an epedemic going around. He was more than just a cousin he was more like a big brother. Before he went to the hospital I looked at his eyes they were big like he couldn't turn them. He kissed my brother and I and told us to be good. He knew he was going to die and so did I in a way but I didn't want to face it. I got my friend to stay with me that night. I when they got back from the hospital I found that they had sent him home with some pills. That night he said that his stomach was aching and my aunt started massaging his stomach. After a while she continued to massage him all of the sudden he said his stomach didn't hurt and that was it he was gone forever. I cried until my eyes left my body. That night after he died I was sent to my God Sister's house for the night. I kept getting push out of the house with 25¢'s $1.00's and 50¢'s. I went down to my friend house and watched them bring the body out in the plastic bag. That made me cry very hard. I went to my godsister's and she tried to soothe my broken heart but she snuck away and cried herself in the bathroom. To this day I still can't believe he is gone and that was in September 5, of 1977 early monday morning on Labor Day. Labor Day will never be any fun again.

Notice the mechanical errors. Often when a writer's energy goes into writing rather than editing there will be many more mechanical errors, spelling mistakes, missing words, etc.

My first reaction to this piece was one of terrible sadness — for Ava, for her family, and for her cousin. I imagined her watching them bring the body out in a plastic bag, and I imagined Ava's godsister bravely trying to soothe her. The details she used, the risk she took in reliving this experience, helped her produce a piece of writing that serves as evidence for her generalization "Life is sometimes painful when someone dies" and forces a reaction from her reader, who now has something concrete to respond to.

Bad day, bad attitude or bad lesson?

Sometimes, I have to admit, students honestly don't care about what they write, and there isn't much I can say to change that attitude.

The Water Fountain
Anonymous, 7

> Today I brought a pair of pliers to school, just in case I had any trouble with my skateboard. The valve on the water fountain was off and leaking. I turned it on but it was still leaking. In the beginning of fourth period I turned it off and on. Mr. H. and Mr. J. thought I made it leak, but I didn't. Luckily I didn't get in trouble.

Something could probably have been done to strengthen this uninspired piece, but I was put off by the author's reaction to my questions: he sat there lethargically, grumpy, stone-faced, when I tried to help. Maybe he was having a bad day. Maybe he couldn't find a subject or thought everything sounded stupid. In any case, I consoled him by saying, "Writing is hard, and sometimes things just don't add up. Don't worry. You'll write again. I have days where I throw away everything I write." This is true, and it's another advantage of having gone through the writing process myself. I know what it's like to have a bad writing day, and I can sympathize with the student's block instead of suspecting that he is trying to get away with not writing in my class.

Sometimes, however, it is clear after you've tried hard to work through things that the student just isn't interested. In this case, better to stop pushing. If I find that a lot of my students have this attitude, it's worth looking at my lessons. Maybe they're confusing, too difficult, or too simple. Maybe the subjects I'm suggesting don't interest the students.

I've had whole classes that wouldn't work. In one class it turned out that everyone wanted to write mysteries. Personally, I'm not interested in mysteries. I find that when students try to write them, they do poor imitations of TV shows or formula superhero tales. So we compromised. During the first part of each class we generated material and gathered details by making lists of scary sounds, places where mysteries might occur, looks on terrified faces, and actual frightening experiences. After that, everyone went and wrote their mysteries — using details, of course. Reams of material were generated from then on, and what was once a sullen, dispirited class became a lively one.

Another class was unable to concentrate long enough on the prewriting discussion to make an actual writing lesson possible. To keep the students from growing restless, I dispensed with much of the prewriting discussion and began each period by reading the work from the previous week. The reading led into a short discussion of new subjects, and then the writing began. The focusing work I usually do with the whole class I did instead with individuals, helping them to find subjects and research details. The class became very exciting to me because I saw that the students did not need a lesson or a given subject in order to write. As in all teaching, the writing lesson must be adapted to the abilities of the students.

David Belmar, 8

My uncle was in the hospital from a broken back. That weekend my family and I visited him. His back was in pain and when he moved he felt deep pain, as though he was being stretched. When my mother saw him she kissed him with tears in her eyes and when my brother and I went to shake his hand, he shook it slowly up and down. My sister said, "Ooow, oooow," because she feels pain when someone is already in pain. She kissed him as if he was a bomb, as though if she leaned on the bed the wrong way he would explode, even to kiss him. He got sick and tired of that place and he told the nurse he wanted to leave, so he did.

Looking at the writing, not at the writer

We might assume that a good student wrote this piece, because there are few mechanical errors and no spelling mistakes. But the writing process takes place on levels other than those where academically able students tend to succeed, and I cannot assume that some students' writing will be weak because their other academic work is weak, just as I can't assume that my more facile students will be inspired in their writing. Since everyone has experiences and responses to those experiences, most students will be able to write with power if I have prepared them by focusing the lesson carefully enough. That's why it is important to look past poor handwriting, grammar, and spelling to the content of the piece.

The above story was in fact written by a student who had problems with grammatical skills. Here is the piece as it was originally written.

David Belmar

> My uncle was in the hospital from a broken back and call us when he was in the hospital so that weekend me and my family visit him. His back was in pain and when he move he feeled deep pain like if he was in a stretcher. When my mother seen him she kiss him with tears in her eyes and when me and my brother went to shake his hand he shook it slow up and down and then my sister said oooow, oooow because she feels pain when somebody is already in pain So she kiss him like if he was a bomb like if she lean on the bed the wrong way he'll explode but to even kiss him. and he got sick and tired of that place so he told the nurse that he wanted to leave so he did.

Note that though it is full of mechanical errors, all the power, clarity, and precision of feeling that moved us in the corrected piece are here, despite the student's lack of grammatical facility. We must look at the writing to see what is there, not at grades, grammatical abilities, or our own expectations of the writer.

Giving up the role of critic

There are times when it is better not to criticize a piece at all — times when the students have truly done their best for the moment, or times when I'm tired or don't know exactly how to approach the hugeness of a story's problem. There are also times when a piece of writing is, in first-draft form, so rich and inventive that though it may need minor changes or cuts, I want to respond to it as a reader and not as a teacher or critic.

Winds Rain
Dimitri Georges, 3

> When the wind blows through my sweater
> it feels like I am gliding
> down from a hill with my huge wings.
> When I step in a puddle
> I feel like a frog by the meadow, all green.
> When I see the rain fall on my face
> it is like a wet towel on me.
> The sky is as gray as dust.
> The great open sky is an eye crying.
> It travels to my heart like a ball of fire.
> It sets me into flames.

My slow steps make me feel
like a turtle in the dark.
My mind is set free from the cage in my body.
I feel empty, like an old bag in the basement.
When the water falls it's like army ants
travelling for food.
When I go in my house
I am like a bear in its cave.
The loud *boom* explodes my head to another world.
I feel smooth and soft in my bed
while the thunder roars outside.
The lightning is like a lamp
opening and shutting.
My spirit is rising out of me
to another place, a place
where trees and grass are green,
sky and water blue.
The sunlight fights it's way through the clouds.
The rain is over. Trees are bare.
The ground is brown. The streets are flooded.
Yes, the storm is over, over with misery, agony
and most of all with feelings.

The way we respond to students' writing is very important. As critics we can make them feel strong or weak, safe or unsafe in the writing process. How they feel about writing is, over the long run, more important than the success of a single piece. It is this attitude in ourselves and our students that we must try to nourish.

THE TEACHER AS EVALUATOR

When teachers make the assumption that only papers they have read and commented on constitute worthwhile learning experiences, they put a heavy burden both on themselves and on their students. Already overloaded with paperwork, they feel obliged to face thirty more papers each time they give a writing assignment, and given this pressure, they may understandably cut short opportunities for writing in class.

The fact is, learning *does* go on without a teacher's constant evaluation. Practice is the backbone of the craft of writing, and practice means plenty of room to experiment, make mistakes, just write. When a student has little opportunity to write because the teacher has little time for evaluation, that student gets the idea that practice is not necessary in order to write well and that writing is something one does for the teacher and not for oneself.

One way of giving students the opportunity to write freely and also relieving yourself of the burden of constant evaluation is to have them keep journals. A journal is a private notebook, bought or made, in which students can write or draw anything. Privacy, one of the most important factors, makes the journal instantly valuable. While some students may want to share their entries with friends or with you, they know this is not required. Journals are best used daily for five to fifteen minutes. If you can't spare that much class time, however, any amount of time is better than none.

The teacher's most important role in this journal writing is to make sure that everyone has something to write about, since the dilemma of not having a subject will make a student immediately hostile toward the journal. When I first introduce and explain journal writing, the students brainstorm a list of genres and subjects they might write about: stories, poems, letters, inventions, feelings, daily events, memories, comic book plots with their own made-up characters. I suggest they keep these lists in their journals in case they can't think of anything to write. Every few weeks we renew the lists and keep them active.

Sometimes students need help in breaking down the subjects on the list so they are more concrete and accessible. Imagine that the word *feelings* is on the list. This topic is so general that it may not trigger ideas. I have the class brainstorm specific emotions. Now we have the emotion *excited* on the board. It too is a general topic. I ask the students, "What are some different ways you could write about excitement?" They come up with the following concrete suggestions: write about a time you were excited; tell how you act when you are excited; write about the things that make you excited; explain how you feel inside when you are excited. I point out that any emotion can replace *excited*, and we practice making substitutions. These ideas can go onto big charts so that they are available for any student who needs a subject for journal writing. It may be helpful to put a daily topic on the board. It must be clear that these lists and charts and daily topics are just aids, not assignments, and that the students are free to ignore them.

I want to distinguish a journal from what I have heard called a "Daily Log." In the Daily Log students write one sentence on each of an appointed set of subjects: the day's weather, their moods, what they watched on TV, etc.

Obviously this exercise has nothing to do with writing and reflects a mistrust and misunderstanding of both writing and students.

The results of keeping a journal vary. At the least, students tend to feel more comfortable putting words on paper and are less likely to freeze up when they are supposed to write. Some develop a personal use for writing and begin to look forward to it. Little by little they may transfer the writing and editing skills they are practicing in class to their journal writing. And all this learning and understanding and excitement without a minute spent on grading!

While students' writing does not need to be and should not always be under scrutiny and subject to grading, it *can* be evaluated. Writing is not an easily quantifiable process, but it is also not an uncontrolled landslide of feelings. It is a craft. It involves specific skills. This means that students can improve their writing in tangible ways; given specific tools, focused lessons that respond to their abilities and interests, lots of practice, and time, they will become better writers. It does not mean, however, that the second piece of writing will be better than the first, or the third better than the second. It takes time to absorb the elements of writing, and the success of a particular piece depends on many variables. But in the course of the year, your students will gradually move towards more detailed writing, better writing. In this connection, it is important to evaluate students in relation to themselves, not in relation to a standard of age or grade level. Otherwise they will feel like failures and refuse to write, or they will become complacent and feel they know everything.

Throughout this book I have stressed the importance of separating the writing process from the editing process. In making this separation I have not intended to create a dichotomy between the two processes. While a writer may produce page after page of unedited false starts and rough drafts, the final manuscript is neat and legible, checked carefully for correct grammar, punctuation and spelling.

Students must be encouraged to put the editor aside while they write, but the editor can be invited back once a piece is down on paper and ready for the revision and correction necessary to make it accessible to the reader. The question of how to integrate the writing process and the editing process in the classroom is a large one. How do you teach students substantive revision? When do you teach students the mechanics of grammar, punctuation and spelling? How do you help students understand that while these mechanics sometimes may be tedious to learn, they are an important part of the total writing process? The answers to these questions are complex. While my primary goal in this book is to explore the writing process, I would like to offer several suggestions that begin to address these issues.

If you look at the lessons you did in Part I and the ones that follow, you will notice that many are based on, or have as an important element, a syntactical or grammatical concept such as verbs or tenses or sequence. It is possible to devise lessons that highlight sentence structure, dialogue, and various elements of grammar. For example, I asked a class of third graders to share the orders they were given by teachers and members of their family at school or home, at religious services, in a restaurant or at someone else's house. The advantage of teaching the concept in this way is that it uses what students might know but have not yet classified. Students are very aware that they are told what to do; they probably tell others what to do. However, they may not know that this type of sentence is called an *order*. Almost everyone had something to share during this lesson, and the poems were very lively—full of orders!

Orders That People Give Me
George Quinones, 3

George, clean up your room!
  I am sick and tired of you
  telling me what to do!
Stop eating so much!
  I want to shoot that person!
  I want to stab myself!
  I want to kick you!
  I want to stab the chair!
  I hate everyone who gives me orders!
  So, don't, give, me, orders!
George, do your work!
  r,r,r,r,r,m,m,m.

Remember, however, that even in lessons where your objective is to teach a grammatical concept, the writing comes before the editing. If students have trouble writing in present tense, for example, let them write in the way that feels most comfortable. The erosion of their joy in writing will make the lessons useless anyway.

One way to bring editing into the classroom is to have students listen to themselves as they read their own work. Careful listening often reveals where a detail needs to be added or a mechanical error eliminated. Students often make errors not out of ignorance but because they are channeling their energy into the writing. By learning to read, not what they *intended* to write, but what they actually did get on paper, they can catch many of these errors. Once students can read their own work and hear where changes need to be made, they can become editors for each other.

Finally, everything students write does not have to be taken to the editing stage. Let them choose a favorite piece from their writing folders and concentrate on developing that piece into one that is full of details, neat, and mechanically proficient. Posting, publishing, or sharing writing in some public way is an important incentive in developing the desire for precision in this last stage of the writing process.

Grammar and punctuation are valuable tools for writers. They offer ways to approach a subject from a new point of view, to unearth new information, to be more precise and to moderate the pace and tone of a piece of writing. Recently, the editing process has been perceived as dangerous because too often it is mistaken *for* the writing process. The way a piece looks, its "correctness," becomes more important than content or the spirit of invention. We need to continually work to make the distinction between writing and editing clear to ourselves and our students. The editor who comes to work *after* a piece has been written is a valuable ally to any writer.

THE WRITING LESSON

The last part of this book presents thirteen lessons which treat various writing elements and subjects yet share a standardized format. I have divided the lesson into four phases: Generating Material/Gathering Details, Stating the Topic, the actual Writing Time and a Time for Sharing. Within these phases I have described the specific teaching techniques you will need.

Generating Material/Gathering Details

The generating of material, or brainstorming, serves two important functions at the beginning of class. It provides a bridge from everyday concerns to writing concerns, and it provides a time to generate excitement and a range of ideas broad enough to spark individual tastes and interests. This time is like a group freewriting exercise during which students absorb skills, consider, connect, discard ideas, and come to focus on what they will write about. The principles of brainstorming apply here: allow enough time to develop a range of ideas, and reserve judgment so that every idea has a chance. This process works only if the students themselves are generating the material. It does *not* work if I am telling them their range of possibilities.

Asking questions to get a range of material

Associating, breaking down, and finding categories are skills we all use, often without realizing we are using them. When ideas are coming slowly or are not broad enough, these techniques can help get things moving.

In associating, one idea suggests another. For example, in brainstorming places, someone says, "Gym." I might then ask the students if a gym reminds them of other places.

In breaking down, a place like gym is separated into its component parts, producing a new cluster of ideas. I might say, for example, "A gym is a large place. What are some particular places in a gym?" Students might suggest the locker room, the basketball court, the track.

When the suggestions being made are too narrow, I use the opposite of breaking down: finding categories. A detail may suggest a category that in turn opens up a range of ideas. For example, still working on places, a student proposes, "Bedroom." I ask, "Can you think of other places where people sleep?" The students then suggest tents, hallways, the beach.

I often put these suggestions on the board so that students can see the abundance of their ideas and refer to them if they need to.

Gathering details/focusing

When I sense that the students have a range of material broad enough to trigger a variety of subjects, and that they in fact have subjects they want to share, we begin to focus on specific subjects to help the students understand the lesson. If they are recalling a memory of a time they were in a new place, I ask them to visualize that memory. Where were they when the incident occurred? Can they see that place? What do they notice around them, what smells, noises, objects? How are other people moving? Can they hear conversation? What are they doing or saying, and what is going through their minds? Then, for as long as time allows, I ask students to share their memories. I ask questions to elicit details so that the memory becomes clearer. The other students see for themselves how the details make the speaker's memory visible to those of us who were not there. They hear the kind of questions they can ask themselves when they write. They begin to absorb a sense of the importance of details.

At this point you may find that the lesson takes a direction other than the one you intended. For example, I wanted one class to explore different parts of their hands. They were intrigued with the lines in their hands. As hard as I tried to get them to look at their nails or thumbs, they continued to talk about these lines. It was a choice between my lesson and their fascination, so I changed direction and followed them.

Asking questions to get at the emotional center

Once we have a clearly focused subject, I want to explain the difference between generalizations and details and show the students the power details have. I take the subject and ask questions to pull out the details.

Imagine that a student has said she was once thrown into a pool, not knowing how to swim, and was scared. Here I am particularly interested in the details around the emotional center of the situation, the details that disclose the strongest feelings in the memory. For such a short memory I don't care how the student got in the pool or what happened later. I am interested in helping her find the details she can use to *show* us her fear so she can do more than tell us, "I was scared." I might ask questions like "What were you doing immediately before you were thrown into the water? What did you notice as you were being thrown in? Did you see the water coming toward you? What else did you notice? Do you remember your thoughts? Do you remember hearing anything? Do you remember hitting the water? What did the water feel like? Did you want to do something? What did you do? How were you moving in the water? If you can't remember clearly, tell us what you think you remember, or make it up. In writing, we can make up things to go in our stories even if they don't represent exactly what happened."

Through my questions I am trying to help pull into the open specific details that were experienced powerfully and will therefore give the writing power. I don't necessarily ask all these questions, and if the student offers information that I consider relevant to the emotional center, I don't discount it. She may or may not use these details successfully in her writing. My questions are intended to help the student remember more details, not to dictate how the memory must be written.

When the student's story is rich with detail, I retell the first, general version and the second, more specific version. Then I ask the class, "Which story is better? Which do you best like listening to? In which can you really see what happened?" The answer is inevitably the second. In this way the students can see for themselves how details give writing power. By listening to a classmate probe her memory, they learn how to explore their own memories.

Asking questions to get precise details

I am always trying to help students see more precisely. A child says, "Hello flower." I say, "Look at that flower in your mind. Can you tell us something about it, the color of the flower or how it moves?" "Hello pink flower. " That's not much of a detail, but it's a start.

A student says, "I'm happy when I get a present." "What present," I ask, "makes you happy?"

"I feel sad when someone dies." "Are you thinking of someone who died?" "I feel sad because my uncle was shot."

I am always after the detail, asking questions to get to the precise flower, the precise present, the precise reason for sadness.

Asking questions to extend details

Do you remember when we were extending comparisons in Part I? I said first that my hand, when it was stretched back, looked like a wave. Then I wanted to make that image more precise, because after all, the wave could be hitting the rocks or rolling across the sand, so I looked again and saw that my hand stretched back looked like a wave that had just reached its crest and was about to break.

I also use questions to help the students extend their images, make them more precise.

"When I can't think my mind is like a wall." "Look at that wall," I say. "See it inside your mind and tell us more about it."

"When I'm excited I'm like a bomb." "Pay attention to that bomb inside you. Really feel it. What do you notice about that bomb?"

"My arm is like a bridge." "What is the bridge connecting?" I ask. "My arm is like a bridge connecting my body with all of the space in the world." The exact image, the concrete detail, gives a piece of writing its structure and power.

What if everyone says the same thing?

Sometimes an answer is very attractive. It is an answer other students immediately relate to and want to offer themselves. In one class I was doing a collaborative poem in which we were saying hello to things. One student said hello to her friend Jennifer. The next student I called on also said hello to a friend. I could see we were headed for trouble, so I asked, "How many of you would like to say hello to your friend?" All of them raised their hands. "Good," I said, and wrote in the poem, "Hello to my friend from all of us." I read it to them and then said, "Now that we've all said hello to our friends we can go on and say hello to other things."

But besides using on-the-spot invention, there are certain questions I can always ask to suggest to students that they have other things to say: for example, "Does anyone want to share a different idea?" I ask questions to help guide students to different ideas because if they can't think of anything about a squirrel except that it's brown, that's all they will say. I ask specific questions: "What about the tail, the eyes, the fur?" This technique sets the students' minds working, and they generate a variety of ideas. It is much more successful than screaming in desperation, "Stop saying the same thing!"

On the other hand, I discourage students from thinking that a topic one has chosen is off limits for another: "Hey, he took my subject." "What is your subject?" "The time I fell off my bike." "There are a lot of ways to fall off a bike."

Writing a collaborative poem

A collaborative poem is a poem written by the group, each person's response being added to it. A collaborative poem is a good way to illustrate a lesson if there is too little time for individual writing or if you have a class where students can't write. It helps the students actually see and demystify the writing process: their thoughts are spoken and written down on paper or on the blackboard, and they can see that nothing mysterious happens to the words on the way.

In a collaborative poem I try to accept all ideas and, as always, ask the students questions that will help them give a detailed response. In the following poem, each idea was contributed by a different student.

The Cold
Second-Third-Grade Class,
P.S. 50, Manhattan

When my body gets cold I feel like an ice cube. I like to feel cold.
When I am cold I turn into a freezer. My heart stops beating
    and I die. My mother opens the freezer and says, "What you
    doin' in there, boy?" My mother takes me out and puts me in
    a pot and I melt.
When I get hit by a snowball my skin feels like it's oozing blood.
When the wind blows my face gets cold. I think my face will break.
When my face gets cold it turns red as fire.
When my ears get cold they ring as if 402 bells are in my head.
When I walk in snow my feet get cold. I ball them up and they
    feel like giant goose bumps.
When my feet are cold it feels like frost bugs have crawled into
    my boots and then into my shoes. I start falling down.
When my feet are cold one toe climbs on top of another.
Ice water gets in my shoes. My feet freeze.
My cold ears feel crunchy.
I put my cold feet in hot water. The hot water tickles my feet
    and I get warm, warm, warm.

Telling a group story

Like a collaborative poem, a group story is made up of responses from all the students. I generally do these stories orally, sometimes taping them so the students can hear them when they're complete. Group stories are a good basis for class books. Each child can illustrate a part of the story and give the picture a caption.

Group stories are good thinking exercises since, the students have to take more and more facts into consideration as the story progresses. They are also good practice for listening, problem solving, and on-the-spot invention.

Stating the Topic

Often I can tell that a class is ready to write by the number of students who have ideas they want to share or by the amount of sharing going on in the class. If I am not sure whether the class is ready to write, I ask how many students have their ideas. If very few do, we continue generating material. Sometimes I ask those who have ideas to share them, and this seems to provide peer incentive for the others to find an idea.

When enough material has been generated, enough details have been gathered, and the idea of the lesson is clear, I ask the students to sit quietly and see their subject in their minds, see it in detail. I restate the writing topic. I remind them not to worry about grammar, punctuation, or penmanship, but to put all their energy into the writing, to write their story just as if they were telling it out loud to the class. I remind them that if they don't have a subject right away, they can take some time to sit quietly, look at the ideas on the board, and daydream. Sometimes, I explain, it takes time to settle on a subject. I add that if after a few minutes I see they're having a hard time, I'll be happy to help them find a subject. Then they start writing.

Writing

Helping when a student can't find a subject

If a student can't find a subject, I ask if I can help. I apply the same technique I use to generate material with a class: I ask a range of questions. Often one question will get the student started: "Look at your finger. What does it remind you of?" "While we were talking did you have a particular memory?" "Let me read you some of the ideas on the board and see if they spark an idea." If one question isn't enough, try to narrow the range of choice: "Would you rather write about sadness or excitement?" "Would you rather start out looking at your palm or your veins?" "Would you rather write about a problem at school or at home?" The words may trigger an idea that has nothing to do with my suggestions, and that's fine. The point of my questions is to spark an idea that engages the student.

Maybe the narrowing process has to go further. The student wants to write about a problem at home, but what problem? Rather than "What problems do you have?" I ask, "Do you want to write about problems you have with *somebody* or *something*?...Okay, who lives in your house?...Would you rather write about problems with your father or your sister?...What problems do you have with your sister?" The questions keep getting more and more focused until the student arrives at a subject.

Sometimes I go quite far with my questioning and the student still doesn't have a subject. I check to see if there is some distraction: "Is something on your mind? Do you want to write about that?" I suggest writing about not being able to get an idea: "What does your blank mind feel like? What would you like to say to your mind?"

Sometimes I have to give up, but helping a student is generally not so hard. If the student can just get some words on paper, ideas usually start flowing.

Helping when a student doesn't know how to write about the subject

If a student has an idea but doesn't know how to write about that idea, I ask particular questions to help find a focus, just as I do with the class. I ask to hear the idea, and often that is all that's necessary to get the student started. If the subject is too broad, I ask a question that triggers a specific detail: "Where exactly did this memory happen?" "Is there something about this place you always notice?" If necessary, I continue asking questions to help pull out details.

Helping students who have difficulty getting words on paper

If students write so laboriously that it's torture for them to compose, I let them dictate their stories to me. They can then copy what I write, and little by little they will tackle the project of writing themselves. If they can't write because they are afraid they will "do it wrong" or won't be able to get help if they need it, I alternate with them, writing every other line. Usually after sharing the writing once or twice, students are fine on their own.

Correcting student concepts

To me, teaching writing is an opportunity to see into a person's mind. The reality of a student's vision is more important to me than the "correctness" of that vision. When Jennifer writes, "I want to help people who get killed by fire," I am not interested in teaching her that people who are killed cannot be helped. That can be done another time. I am interested in the intensity of her desire to help people. That is what writing is: a person's understanding of herself and the world around her.

Trusting students; helping them trust themselves

Sometimes students complain to me, "I don't know how to start." In fact, when I ask if they have any idea, it turns out that they have a very clear notion of how they want to begin; they are just unsure that it is the *correct* way. I encourage students to go with their ideas, to trust their impulses. Sometimes students ask if they can approach a subject from a point of view that hasn't been discussed. Again, I encourage them to trust their reaction and go with their inclination.

Sharing

If it is lonely to leave the excitement of the group for the solitude of the paper, if it is a struggle to pull out the words for what you know so well in your thoughts, it all becomes worthwhile when you share what you have written. Making sure that the students have an opportunity to share their work is crucial to the continued spirit of the writing lesson.

At the least, student papers should be read aloud, by the writer or the teacher, depending on the time available or the reading ability or shyness of the writer. This may seem like not much to ask, but often you will have spent so much time generating material, gathering details and writing that very little, if any, is left for sharing. I encourage students to share their work among themselves when they finish writing. I am also working to discipline myself so I leave time for sharing.

I can't overemphasize the importance of reading students' work. This is an exciting time in the class and everyone looks forward to it. In fact, I have found that when there is not time for sharing over a long period, the students begin to get lethargic about their work. As one student said to me once, "What's the use of writing if no one is going to read it?" I always try to read the pieces smoothly and with expression, as if the piece were completely edited. I want the students to feel pride in their writing, even in their attempt to write! I want them to see that their words often evoke a response from their classmates. This is less likely to happen if I am pointing out mistakes or stumbling over missing words.

After a piece has been read, if there is time, the members of the audience and I can help the writer by pointing to particular details that stand out to us; we can offer a response to the whole piece and describe how it moved us; we can ask for clarification of parts we didn't completely understand. This kind of sharing may lead the writer to rewrite the piece or extend it. It helps develop the critical abilities of both writer and audience.

Generally, the more opportunities writers have to share their work, the more pride and energy they will put into both writing and editing. Therefore it is extremely worthwhile to develop as many outlets as possible for sharing the writing: class readings, posting of work on bulletin boards, class and school publications, community activities, etc.

THE TEACHING LESSONS

HOW TO USE THESE LESSONS

In this section you will find thirteen lessons and numerous variations that adapt the skills and processes you used in the workbook to the classroom situation. You may only want to dip in and out of them; you may feel comfortable going into the classroom with your own lessons, or you may want to take the sequence of lessons you did in the workbook and tailor them for classroom use.

The lessons do not need to be done in any specific order. I generally begin a class by introducing the concept of detail, but you may find a different start works better for you and your class. The last three lessons are geared to older children, although they can be adapted for younger grades.

The lessons run from forty-five minutes to over an hour, depending on the amount of time available. However, the less time you have, the more likely it is that sharing will be left out.

Each student should have a folder specifically for writing purposes. An X at the top of the paper indicates that the writing is private and should not be read to the class.

The example

I begin each lesson in this section with an example of the type of poem that may be generated by the lesson. You may want to use this example and/or the poems at the end of each lesson to help your students generate ideas. Remember, however, that the example is not the "perfect poem" to be produced from the lesson and that students should not feel compelled to imitate it.

The lesson

I have set up the lessons in two columns. The column on the right approximates what I say to the students. The hypothetical examples I give represent the types of replies you may get.

The column on the left contains my notes to you. They are shorthand reminders of the material in the previous section, "The Writing Lesson."

Though you have done variations of most of these lessons in the first part of this workbook, I suggest that you always try a lesson before giving it to the class so you can anticipate difficulties and be certain that the subject is appropriate and the question works. In the classroom it is necessary to be flexible. These lessons are based on what works for me most of the time, but I do have to vary them according to the age, ability and mood of the group.

Each lesson is divided into the four stages discussed in "The Writing Lesson": Generating Material/Gathering Details, Stating the Topic, Writing, and Sharing.

Anthology

For each lesson and variation I have selected poems and stories that illustrate the *range of writing* students produce. Your students will produce writing that is both different from and similar to these examples.

The number after the name of each writer indicates grade level at the time the piece was written, but it is not a guide for what an eighth grader or a fourth grader should be writing. The quality of a student's work depends on the strength of the lesson and the concentration, interest, and ability of the student.

These poems can be used in the classroom. I include them also because of all they can teach. I have found that the students' writing, whether strong or weak, has been my greatest resource in becoming more and more sensitive as a writer, a reader, and a teacher. Looking at the writing from the points of view presented in "Teacher as Critic" (p. 95), I have come to see how particular lessons encourage invention and energetic response while others fail to trigger anything genuine in the students. I have come to trust the intelligence and sensitivity of the writer, and I have become a more responsive and careful reader. I highly recommend these poems and your own students' work as an enjoyable and instructive lesson in writing.

Through reading so much student work I have also come to the realization that I cannot expect thirty extraordinary poems from a class of thirty writers. I have had to relieve myself and my students of the burden of responding with brilliant invention and insight each time they write. The danger of keeping this expectation is that both the students and I will fail so often that we will quit before we have had time to understand, absorb, and perfect our writing and the teaching of writing.

Variations

There are only thirteen lessons here, but they deal with such basic writing subjects that with simple substitutions of object, place, memory, etc., they can easily generate a career's worth of ideas. In each lesson I suggest some of these variations.

Once you feel comfortable with writing techniques such as metaphor, tense, point of view (first, second, third person), and voice, you will have even more variations, since any subject can be viewed from these different perspectives to produce new insights.

Moreover, once you feel comfortable with the structure of the writing lessons and with helping students generate material, gather details, and focus their ideas, you will find that classroom events lead naturally into writing. Your students' poems and stories will spark many new ideas.

The students will also lead you to new lessons and variations on old ones by their interest and curiosity. Don't be scared of this, and don't be afraid to try something new just because the writing lesson might not work or you might get stranded in a place you don't know how to get out of. Just remember to trust the prewriting preparation, details, and the excitement and talent of your students. You'll find that at worst, the lesson, and therefore the writing, will lack focus or be confused. At best, you and your class will discover something new about yourselves and writing. Whether you end up with the best, the worst, or something in between, you will be observing the spirit of writing: taking risks and letting your curiosity take the lead in helping you look at something from a new point of view.

LOOKING OUT A WINDOW: PLACE

**Looking Out Our
Bedroom Window**
Shizu Homma, 5

> I lie on my bed on my back.
> I see blue sky and gigantic white, cool, soft clouds.
> I imagine LITTLE TWIN STARS on one of them. I see
> part of the roof, made of reddish-brownish-blackish
> bricks. I imagine myself jumping from cloud
> to cloud and I land, and the cloud goes in. And the
> sun is shining, not so hard, just medium-rare.

Generating Material/Gathering Details

Is there a window in your house you like to look out of? Maybe it's your bedroom window or kitchen window; the window in your parents' room or the room of the person who takes care of you; the bathroom or living room window or a window I haven't mentioned.

Generate a range of ideas.

Can some of you tell us where your favorite window is? And do you stand at that window? Lie down? Sit on a chair or a couch?

Help students gather details by letting them visualize what they see out their window.

Now picture yourself at that window. Look out the window. What do you see? If you see people, what are they doing? If you see an animal, what is it doing? If you see the sky, see everything you can about it.

What do the things you see out your window make you think or wonder about or imagine?

Who would like to share what they saw and wondered about as they looked out their window?

Ask questions to gather details.

You saw a cat on the fire escape. Where were you? Tell us about that cat. Did you notice anything about its face? How was it moving? Did seeing that cat make you think or wonder about something? Imagine something? Can you share that with us?

Have as many students as possible share what they see to generate excitement and an understanding of details.

Does someone else want to tell us what they see out their window?

Stating the Topic

Get very quiet and in your mind see yourself at a window you really like to look out of. What exactly do you see? What does this sight make you think or imagine or wonder?

Don't worry about how to start. Just tell us what you see, as if you were talking to us. Don't worry about your grammar, punctuation or spelling. Concentrate on writing what you see out this window.

Writing

Be sure every student has a subject. Ask, What window do you like to look out of?

When necessary, help students gather more details.

Sharing

Have students take turns reading their pieces aloud, or read them yourself.

What detail really stands out to you in this piece? Which detail do you really like?

Anthology and Variations

Justo Fuentes, 4

Yesterday I saw out the window
and I saw cars driving to their work,
nurses walking to the hospital,
and men walking to their jobs.
I stood looking from my window two hours
and it was fun. I liked the way
the people were going
to their good jobs.

Jed Smith, 4

I wake up late Saturday morning. I go downstairs. I sit on my knees and look out the window in my mother's room. I look at one tree and everything goes away except the tree, and I shake my head and then I see and hear everything again. I look at my brother's sandbox. I look at the little hill in my backyard. I look at the fig tree. I see the same thing every morning. And then I hear my mother yell, "Jed, it's time for breakfast. What would you like, eggs or hot cereal?" I answer, "I'll have eggs," and I go downstairs and I begin my day.

Nicole Joos, 5

I am looking out the window of my door. I see Snapdragon, our grey tiger-striped cat. She is arguing with another cat. Her tail puffs up. She makes herself look scrawny and sick. The cat she is arguing with is a full-grown grey cat. Snapdragon moves forward; the strange cat turns around and threatens her to come closer. Snapdragon moves forward again but jumps back immediately because the other cat hisses and sticks its paw out. "Go, Snap, go!" I scream, although I don't even want them to fight. Snapdragon walks to the door. I let her in. "Are you hungry, Snaparoo, roo, roo?"

Window Stories
Martin Segarra, 8

I. Looking out of the window I look to the left. Then I look to the center. I look to the right and BANG! A car crash in the highway and the car turns over. I look to see if anybody is hurt but I can't see. It is dark.

I could count how many car crashes happen in the same place. The same place over and over. I know the reason. I saw. About five months ago there was the first car crash right in the same place on the F.D.R. Drive and oil smeared all over. Now whenever it rains the oil gets slippery and cars go fast through there. I can see the oil getting wet and cars zooming by—and cars crashing. That day I could see that man suffering in that car.

II. I am thinking. I'm looking out the window—if those kids fall down while a car is coming by. . . . Sometimes I wonder how birds can fly. How can they get off the ground? It looks impossible when a pigeon or a sparrow takes off. I wonder what it would be like if we had wings. Imagine if I could just jump out this window and fly instead of taking those elevators that keep getting stuck. Just imagine how many people would be flying back and forth. Sometimes I imagine too much. I get carried away. Sometimes I imagine and wonder and sometimes it all comes up true.

III. I wonder, I wonder if someone ever walks in and says, "I think this group is wonderful. I'm going to sponsor you." And we become famous. Just think how all the things we ever imagined would come possible. We would write books, publish them. Just imagine all the crazy thoughts I have. What if we go to sell books and all the elementary kids decide our books are wonderful. I wonder if I could write magic stories that would make people want to buy our books. Imagine how Barbara would feel. Wonderful.

IV. I'm trying to think—what is this scratching noise I hear? Is it hungry rats? What is it? "Scratch, scratch, scratch." I think it's coming from the other room. I'm walking to the hall and staring at the front door. Is there a robber trying to get in? I hear scratching again. It's coming from my sister's room. I stare at her door. Is it my sister? No, my sister is downstairs. I'm thinking, What if I open the door and someone jumps on me? I see a shadow. The scratching stops. The door begins to open very slowly. It makes a squeaky wicked noise. I move back. I think. I run to my room. Should I get a bat? My pool stick? I think fast and I grab my bat. I run to my sister's room and the door is still opening. Just as it opens I think fast and I swing down but then I think even faster because it is my dog. What a relief it is to think on time. I would have hit my dog. I would have killed him. I go and look at the wall in my sister's room and there's a big hole there. What if my father sees this? He will throw my dog out. I take my dog and hit him. I walk back out the door, put my bat in my room and close the door of my sister's room so Justice, my dog, won't open the door with her mysterious paws.

121

V. Looking out of the window I see many people having problems and I also see that they can't handle their problems. Some have mental problems. Most problems come from alcohol and smoking. I wonder how I'm going to handle these problems if I ever happen to fall into one. I have many thoughts of my future. "Many thoughts!" I see situations with people who don't have money to support their family. I see people in jail. Am I ever going to be in jail? Am I going to suffer? I wonder all these things of my future which is not far away from where I am. I hope when my problems come to me or I go to them that these problems that are not that far away from here are not complicated problems, for I know everyone gets problems. As the years pass and the days go and the hours go and the minutes pass and the seconds go I wonder how I'm going to handle all my problems.

Variation:
Describe a place you particularly like or dislike.

My Life in the Bathroom
Tanya Diaz, 4

When I am in the bathroom
it feels like somebody is there.
I touch the shower curtain.
I look at it.
In one second I am seeing things,
stars and circles.
When I get out my mother talks to me
and I do not hear anything
she is saying. For example,
she tells me to go and eat.
I just don't hear her;
and when I am wandering round
I just dip my hand in the cake mix,
just to taste it,
and then I snap out of it.
When I go and wash my hands and face to eat
it feels like somebody is going to touch me
and I touch the door and bounce up.
When I am taking a bath
it looks like somebody is watching me.
I stand still
The next thing I know I am out of the bathtub.
and I am thinking, "What happened? Where am I?"
I am supposed to be in the shower. Then my father tells me
how I stepped out of the tub.

In the Locker Room
Dailah Vargas, 8

I walked into the locker room, screamed, "Is anyone in here?" There was no response. I turned the lights on. I walked slowly down an aisle. The silence was scary; the only sound was the clonking of my shoes. I walked to my locker, fiddled with my combination. It wouldn't open. I took my shoes off, walked into the bathroom. As I sat down I looked at all the writing, tried to think about my bathroom at home and sort out the beauty of it. As I walked past the mirror I got a chill up my spine. I stopped and wondered if it was the cold dampness of the room that made it happen. I continued back to my locker. Getting it open I hurried to unchange, stopped for a second to smell the prettiness of my clothes and the old, cold smell of the room.

The Statue of Liberty
Iris Rivera, 7

I see hundreds and hundreds of people pushing and bumping into each other. I see the souvenir room crowded with people. I hear the loud echoing of people's feet climbing to the top. People running up the spiral staircase to the head of the statue. The air is polluted with the smell of cigars and no one is able to breathe.

I'm almost at the head of the statue and I am getting tired of climbing all the way to the top. I stop to rest in a corner and then I get up and keep climbing to the top of her head. I walk to one of the windows in the crown and look down to the water. My body sways back and forth as if the statue was going to fall into the waters. She stands tall, holding a book with Roman numerals in her hands and when you look down through her you see that the people look like little ants.

Variation:
If you could be anywhere in the world right now, where would you be?

Fun at the Beach
Lily Sarabria, 8

One day on a Saturday morning at 9:00, Brenda, Nilda and I were going to Coney Island. When we got there nobody was there, but the rides were moving and the food was free. Brenda got very nervous and wanted to run home because she knows rides don't move by themselves; we told her to calm down because she couldn't take the train home by herself. Nilda, Brenda and I had the same clothes on, even the same bathing suits. So we took a swim. After that I got on the roller coaster; Brenda got on the horses and Nilda got on the Water Falls. It was strange because the rides stopped when we went to get on and once we got on they started moving and when we said stop, they stopped. So we got off.

These three guys from Performing Arts were walking in back of us and they each grabbed one of us and we got scared because they said they were robbers. They took us to the water but then one of the guys took Nilda behind a rock and another one took Brenda behind the rides. One of the guys stayed with me in the water and we were happy because the guys liked each of us and we liked them. After that we went for a swim. I asked them, how did they know we were here? My sister had told them.

Nilda and Brenda and I told them we had to be home by 9:00 but we got home at midnight, that's how much fun we had. When we got home we told our parents that we had gone to the movies.

In a Hammock
Olga Marrero, 5

I'm in a hammock in Pennsylvania. I feel the wind blowing. I feel like the wind is taking me to the clouds. I see up in the sky. I tell the wind, no, I can't. I have to stay and see the flowers turn colors and hear the birds singing love songs. Oh wind, stay here like my furry coat and rub my hand. Oh no, here comes that smell again of horse manure. Wind, wind, help blow that smell out of here so my birds can breathe and my flowers can turn colors.

"Olga. Olga, come and eat."
"Wait mom, I'm doing something."
"Well, hurry up."

Look. The flowers, they were red and now they've turned blue and yellow. How amazing. I can't believe it. It's like seeing things. I feel like I'm on another planet, out of orbit. Like heaven talking about heaven. Look at the clouds. They're like smoke up in heaven.

"Olga. Olga!"
"Wait mom, please."
"I'm going to call your father."
"No, wait. I'll go in."

Well, goodbye green trees that remind me of my green pants and goodbye flowers that remind me of a rainbow. Bye. Bye. Bye.

Variation:
You are in bed at night.

Sharonica Portis, 1

I hear a window creaking.
Why are you doing this?
Don't you know I'm sleeping?

Michael Turner, 1

It was at night.
This big rat
came in my bed
and he came to sleep
with me in my bed.
And what nerves
that big rat had!

124

**When I Am Going
to Sleep**
Rose Marie Guichardo, 2

When I am going to sleep
my mother says good night.
Then she puts out the light.
Then the clothes start to dancing
and the cars make music
and the wind gets in the act.
Then my blueberry bear gets out
of his carriage
and then my two Barbie dolls
start to dancing with blueberry bear,
and then I say, Mommy, Mommy.
She comes in and hugs me.
Then I fall asleep.

Nancy Matos, 3

I hear wood falling
and birds flying across the sky.
I go to the edge of the bed
and hear the wind blowing across
and butterflies backing their wings
on my bedroom window.

Miguel Garcia, 3

I hear my blood going through my veins
like a river down a rocky path
and I hear my heart storming down the stairs.

FOCUSING ON A SCENE

Alone in a New City
Dimitri Georges, 3

When my mother said, "We are going back to Haiti," I had a happy feeling. I know I was happy because my stomach tingled. When I arrived, chickens were running in the street, fruits were hanging, farms were near. I took a chicken and kept him like a pet. The trees were completely green. I felt like a bird flying in the sky, and flying high above the sea.

I was sad because I had to go. I know because my heart broke. So as a prize I kept the chicken and I still have him today.

Generating Material/Gathering Details

Encourage a range of ideas by having students remember the various places in which they were new.

Any memory can be substituted for A Time You Were New.

Help students gather details by letting them visualize the memory.

Can you think of a time you were new in a place? New at a school, on a street, in a neighborhood? In a family or country or club? In a place I haven't mentioned?

Maybe you were scared or shy or unhappy or nervous or excited.

Can some of you share what you remember—a place in which you were new?

Would you get very quiet now and try to remember one time you were in a new place. Try to see it in your mind. If you don't have a memory yet, don't worry. Just keep wandering through your memories. Maybe the questions I ask will help you remember a time you were new.

In this memory exactly where are you? What do you see? Are there certain objects you notice? Certain people? Do you hear any particular sounds or smell any particular smells? Look at yourself in this memory. What are you doing? Do you have any feelings in your stomach? Your eyes? Your hands? Are you wondering about something or saying something to yourself?

Have as many students as time allows relate their memories. Ask questions to help them focus their memory, gather precise details and feel the emotional center of the memory.

Can someone share the time they remember and tell us everything you remember about it?

You say you were new in the neighborhood and you were scared because there were a lot of kids there. You probably remember several experiences that occurred while you were new. Are you thinking of one specific incident?

Where exactly were you when this event happened?

Kids came. What did you notice about them? Was anyone else there with you?

You say you felt scared. How did you know you felt scared? Did you have certain feelings in your body? A certain taste in your mouth? Were you moving or standing in a certain way? Did any thoughts go through your mind?

I am asking all of these questions because details are important. Do you remember M's first story? It was this:

I was new in my neighborhood and I was scared of all the kids.

But she knew more that that. When I asked her for specific details she told us more and more. Her second story goes something like this:

I was standing next to the truck and my parents were taking out a couch. I was picking apart a piece of tin foil I had found. When I looked up there was a group of kids looking at me. I almost jumped. I looked for my parents but they weren't back yet. My heart felt like it was drowning and I thought the kids were going to laugh at me.

This is an important question. The length of the second story does not make it better. The focus and the details make it better.

Which story do you like better? Why do you like the second one better?
In the second version M told us everything. We could really see what was happening, and now we know just how she felt. When we write we want to give *all* the details; we want to tell everything so the reader knows just what happened and just how we felt.

Stating the Topic

Now sit back and look in your mind at your memory of being in a new place. You're going to write it just as if you were telling it. Don't worry about spelling or grammar or even your handwriting, as long as you can read it. Focus all of your energy on writing everything you remember about this time.
Get the picture in your mind. See yourself in the place where this memory occurs, the exact place. Do you see it? When you are ready, start writing.

Writing

Be sure every student has a subject. Ask, Have you ever been new in a place?
Help students begin their memory in a specific place.

Sharing

Have students take turns reading their pieces aloud or read them yourself.

Is there one detail in this piece that really stands out to you?
Can you imagine how the author felt? What details tell you?

Anthology and Variations

My First Day in Kindergarten
Talya Bosch, 3

It was sunny out. When I walked in, I was scared. I walked behind the painting easel. I wanted to paint then and there, with no one in the room, but with the teacher looking straight ahead like a dummy. Then I realized that I couldn't do that, so I really was scared. I didn't want to see the kids. I thought I would not make any friends. I was shocked when some of the kids looked similar to me. Some looked different, and I was happy to know, not one was a monster. As a matter of fact, a very big majority were really nice. When school was out I felt good. I made about nine friends.

Variation:
Brainstorm various times.
Choose one as a subject.

The Lost Hamster
Gabrielle Vitiello, 4

One day when I came into school and I walked into the classroom, everybody ran up to me yelling and screaming. I had no idea what they were saying so I just walked away and said to the pet monitor, "How's Browney?" He looked like there was something wrong so I turned around and everybody nodded their heads. I started to cry and I started looking everywhere in the cage. I said to myself, "Browney's gone. The only thing I can do is look." So everyone helped me look and tried to stop me from crying. Then the door opened. My heart started beating. I knew it was going to be Julie. Julie walked in and she came over to me and said, "Why are you crying?" I didn't say anything. I just held her hand and led her to the empty cage. She looked at me and said, "No. It's a dream, right?" No one answered. We just stood there, solid as ice, everything silent. Then she yelled with sadness, "COME ON! DON'T JUST STAND THERE. LOOK!" Everybody looked and looked. The end of the day came and Browney was not found yet. I went home still crying. I went up to my room and went to sleep.

In the morning, when I woke up, I got up as fast as I could and got dressed and brushed my teeth and ran to school. I walked into school very slowly. I walked up the stairs and went very slowly into the classroom. Everyone looked happy. I paid no attention. I just went up to the cage and Browney was not in his cage. I went in the closet and Julie was sitting on a cart holding Browney. I felt myself smile. Julie said, "The P.H. found him running across the rug." I started screaming with excitement.

Variation:
Brainstorm verbs. Let a
verb trigger a memory.

Fight
Steven Grives, 5

On August 15, 1979, in my home at 5PM I was in a fight. My family was just about to eat. My mother and father were setting the table. Brian was watching *Tom and Jerry*. Paul was sulking in his room. His radio was blasting. I had just come in from playing football. My mother called us for dinner. As I walked in front of Paul, I felt a sharp pain in my side. Paul had given me a karate chop. I went flying over the sofa. I was mad. I jumped on his back and started to hit him in the head. He hit me on the back and I dropped off him like a dead fly. I was madder than ever! My breath was hot as fire. My parents walked into the room. They tried to break up the fight. I hit my brother in the face. His glasses fell off. Brian got into the scene. He pounced on Paul's back. Paul hit him. He plopped on the floor. My father dragged him off the scene. The battle still went on. Then Paul's friend came in and saw the fight. He saw the blood dripping out of my nose. He held Paul off! I ran into the bathroom crying. I locked the door. Paul was kicking at the door. I was holding it. I let go! He flew into the bathroom and I ran out. When I came in everything was settled. We finally ate.

My Sloppy Brother
Victor Rios, 5

Do you have a sloppy, slippery brother like my brother? He's real sloppy. He throws my clothes on the floor. He eats bananas and throws the peels on my bed. He comes with his friends and messes up my room. He takes the drawers and throws them. They smash against the wall like thunder. He takes my clothes and throws them on the walls, floor, and in the hall and they fall like rain.

Then my mother comes in the room and all the kids get quiet. My mother makes an excuse. She says to my brother's friends to come another time because we have to study. The minute the door is closed my mother's eyes burn red and my mother's skin turns different colors, blue, red, purple, yellow, tan, gray, and her hand moves very swiftly across my brother's and my face. She takes off her belt and whips the living soul out of us. She hits us with all her might and that little skinny belt burns us. Our skin turns black, blue, purple, yellow, orange, tan, gold, red, white, sky blue, violet, and she tells us to clean our room.

So my brother goes out to play and I start cleaning the room, picking up the drawers, taking the clothes and folding and putting them in my drawers and putting my bed together. Then after I clean that mess my brother did, my mother tells me to take the clothes out of the drawers and iron them. So I slush the clothes on my bed and slush them on the ironing board. Then back and forth I go, swiss, swiss, swiss, and I finish. Instead of folding the clothes, I smush them up in my drawers and I run outside.

I get my brother and push him with great force. He says, "What happened?" I punch him, rip his sweatshirt, twirl his collar, and say, "You better clean this room or I'll rip you lip by lip."

So he does. I take my clothes out and put them down on the floor and say, "You fold and put these clothes in the drawer." He does and I go outside to play and when I come back I am surprised. My room is as shiny as the sun. Now every day I come back from playing outside and my room is shiny as the sun's beam and he never has messed up the room again.

Variation:
Write a memory as if it is happening right now (present tense).

My Performance
Cathy Nesbit, 8

Bump. Bump. Bump.

That's my heart doing that you know. The time is now; I have to go on now. As I look out into the audience I see very familiar faces, and some that are totally strange. I start. I am portraying Sojourner Truth, a black abolitionist. I take a deep breath and exhale to get most of the nervousness out of me. My hands are shaking. I have butterfly fever in my stomach. Blindly, I start getting into the character of Sojourner Truth. I pull my glassless glasses down on the tip of my nose, put my pipe in my mouth and I start again. I hear yells of "Tell em Cathy" and "She's good" and "What's her name?" I am saying, "And ain't I a woman?" and "That man back there says woman can't have as much rights as man because Christ wasn't a woman. Who is your Christ? Where did he come from?" They quiet down to listen to my speech.

I'm aware of it now. I've already started. The people like me, they really do. I kind of like it myself, all the people clapping and smiling. I'm finished and I have pleased my audience. Proud of myself, I take a bow, look into the audience and smile. I'm thinking, "Maybe I'll make a habit of this."

My Route to School
David Adelson, 4

I live on 6th Street between 6th and 7th Avenues. I usually walk on 7th Avenue and go up 13th Street. Okay. Here I am, setting off for school. I try to run up to the corner in 20 seconds. I don't make it. So what? There are exceptions. How about thirty seconds? Yes, that sounds nice. There, I made it in 26 seconds. Well, on with my trip to school. I make it all the way to 9th Street without any red lights. Boy, that was lucky. Here is a red light so I have to wait. The light changes. Good. Now a million cars turn around the corner so I wait for them. Now the light is about to turn again so I have to run to make the light. I count how many station wagons I see to amuse myself. Now I'm at 13th Street and Talim gets off a bus that stops here so we walk up 13th together. We talk about the homework. We get to school and wait on line.

Variation:
Rewrite from the point of view of another character in the memory.

Like Sand, She Slipped
Noreen Boyle, 7

I

A bright, sunny day with relatives and friends. Myself, a shy, young girl watching a tall uncle. The comparison in size made me feel afraid. He was throwing other children into the air and catching them. The sound of laughter was about me. A feeling of loneliness and jealousy crept through me. A small voice inside me asked to be thrown into the air. The uncle, whom I was always too frightened to approach, was overwhelmed that I came to him. His big hands around my waist lifted me higher and higher. I was thrust into the air. The kids were still laughing. I could feel his strong hands grasp for me as I descended. Next was the feel of cement crushing my face. The smell of blood and sounds of screaming. Silence.

The soft warmth of a couch and blanket as my mother placed another icepack upon my head.

II

My Uncle Remembers

The day grew hotter and I longed for an ice cold glass of water. I was to entertain the children while the women were talking, and the others were at the airport waiting for my father's arrival. The restless boys just wouldn't tire. One after the other I would throw them into the air. My arms tired and my hands grew sweaty and slippery. If only they were lighter. It took my entire strength to throw one tiny figure into the air.

I glanced over my shoulder and saw my youngest niece approach me. She stalked over and fixed her wide eyes upon her feet. She quietly stood there until the noise calmed a bit. She asked if I would throw her into the air. Gladly, I bent over and scooped her up. Maybe it was a second wind that came over me, or just the comparison of weight after the boys.

With ease I threw her into the air. It seemed like forever until I reached up and tried to clasp my hands around her little waist. But like sand, she slipped through my sweaty hands. Although it was only a few feet to the ground, it seemed like hours before I heard a thud on the cement. There were many screams from the sidelines, making it hard to determine whether or not she was screaming. Even though I wasn't the one to fall, I was too shocked to move.

THE PARTS OF THE HAND: COMPARISON

Best Hand
Kelly Sayers, 4

In my hand lies a V for Virgo and a sun rising on my thumb. My knuckles are like mountains standing side by side. I can also see a squid swimming for food. The lumps in my hand are like everstopping waves in an ocean. When I flex my hand I can see the world colliding under the ground. When I make my fingers stand up they look like bare trees. When I make a fist my knuckles look like a waterfall. My hands look like roads on a map. When I lick my hand by accident it tastes like salt. Before I cut my nails I look under them and I see an Indian's teepee. Hand, you're the best a guy could ever have.

Generating Material/Gathering Details

This is a good lesson for a collaborative poem.

Today our subject is our hand. It is something we always have with us, yet how closely have we ever looked at it? Today we're going to try to see it as though we'd never seen it before.

Let's begin by listing the different parts of our hand.

Find similes by sparking association, analyzing characteristics, forcing connections.

Now let's choose one of these parts to work with.

What object does your finger remind you of?

What do you notice about your finger? Can you think of something else that has wrinkles like your finger?

Let's say anything—a rug. Can you find a way your finger is like a rug?

You can help a student extend a comparison to make it more visual by asking questions to get more information.

You say your finger reminds you of a branch? Look closely at your finger. Can you tell us more about that branch?

You say a worm has wrinkles like your finger? Look at your finger like it's a worm. What is that worm doing?

You say your finger is like a rug because they both can roll up? Look at your finger rolling up like a rug. Can you tell us anything else about that rug?

Go through this process with several parts of the hand so students understand the concept of comparison and want to try it themselves.

Stating the Topic

Choose either *to* or *about* for younger children.

We've all been looking at our hands. Now you're going to get to look at your own hand and write what you see.

Maybe you want to tell *about* the things you see. You might begin, "My finger is like . . ."

Maybe you want to talk *to* your hand and tell it what you notice. You might begin, "Fingers, you are like . . ."

You can spend all your time on one part or write about several parts.

Don't worry about grammar or spelling. Concentrate on talking to your hand.

Writing

If students are having trouble starting, help them focus on one part of their hand. Ask questions to help extend comparisons.

Help students acknowledge distractions when necessary.

If students aren't comfortable with comparison, let them go wherever their interests and abilities propel them.

Sharing

Have students take turns reading their pieces aloud or read them yourself.

Is there one comparison that really stands out to you?

Are you surprised at how much you saw? Do you like your hand after looking at it so hard?

Anthology

The World in My Hand
Lisa Cabbagestalk, 3

I see veins in my hand.
I see blood in my hand.
I see lines in my hand
and when I push the front of my hand up
I can see a lot of red.
I see knuckles.
I see nails and I see lines on my fingers.
I see branches of a tree in my hand.
I see slanted and wiggly and zigzag
and scary and ugly and happy
and sad things in my hand.
I see everything.
I love looking at my hand.
I see everything in the whole world
in my hand.

My Friend
Julie Mendez, 4

When I'm mad my hand gets up and tickles me
and tries to make me laugh.
I laugh when my hand tickles.
When I'm sleeping my hand gets up
and covers me with the blankets

133

THE PARTS OF THE HAND: COMPARISON

so that I won't get cold.
When my hand hurts I get up
and take my little hand to the hospital
so that my hand can feel better.
My little hand is my pal forever.

My Hand
Marshard Terrell, 3

My hand is strong.
When I have a little paper I can draw big things.

The Mysterious Hand
David Ortiz, 5

When I look at my hand I get scared. So many lines. In, out, over, under. Lines around lines around lines. I begin to think about what would happen if someone shrank. Right on my hand! I wonder if they would get caught in the lines. Imagine being stuck there, struggling for your life.

But they couldn't get out! Slowly my hand would close. They would get loose but the lines would be too high. They would follow the lines but get nowhere for my hand's lines would wind around. It would be like a maze. The more they searched, the more lost they would get. It would be an endless timeless search.

As my hand closed it would get darker. I would open my hand; I would see them lying down. Day after day I would stare, but they would never get up. As the night got darker I would look out the window. My hand would change from birds to bugs to paper and then back to birds again.

I hear a shriek. Then all of a sudden the birds sing, the bugs creep, the paper crumbles. I lie down and fall asleep. When I wake up I look at my hand, but nothing happens.

WHAT MAKES YOU ANGRY: EMOTION

When I Get Huffy!
Akua Hendricks, 4

I get huffy when I can't stay up past my bedtime—that's nine o'clock on the dot exactly—because I want to stay up and watch TV. So...I ask my mother if I can stay up a little bit longer and she says, "No, Akua, it's time for bed." I get so huffy and puffy that I repeat her rudely but I say it low.

This is what I would like to do when I'm ready to see red and beep like a train ready to go off: I want to throw papers, but if I do I will be in hot water, so instead I go under the covers and go to sleep MADLY AND GRUMPY!

Generating Material/Gathering Details

Substitute any emotion. This is a good lesson for a collaborative poem. Generate a range of material.

Ask questions to elicit details.

Ask questions to help the student exaggerate. To encourage honest exploration, don't use this as a time for moralizing.

Collect a range of ideas to generate excitement and an understanding of the lesson's structure.

What makes you angry? Do you ever get angry at people you don't know? With things you own? With yourself? When?

You say it makes you mad when someone bothers you. What exactly do they do to bother you?

What do you feel like doing or saying when you are angry like that? Really exaggerate if you want to. Writing or saying what you would like to do is different from actually doing it.

You feel like saying something to that person. What would you like to say? Would you say it in a certain tone of voice?

What do you do or say instead?

Does someone else want to share what makes them angry? Maybe it's something completely different.

Stating the Topic

We're going to think, through our writing, about ourselves and our anger. What makes you angry? Things at home, at school, or outside? Things your family, friends, strangers or animals do? Things you do to yourself?

What does that anger make you want to do or say? Don't be afraid to exaggerate to help you get the feeling of your anger across.

Do you do or say this or do you do something else instead?

Really let us see you. Give us details so we can feel just how angry you are. Don't worry about spelling or grammar. Concentrate on your writing.

You might want to write one thing that makes you mad or several things.

Writing

Be sure every student has a subject. Ask, What makes you angry? What do you want to do then? Help students be precise in their details.

135

WHAT MAKES YOU ANGRY: EMOTION

Sharing

Have students take turns reading their pieces aloud or read them yourself.

Is there a detail here that really stands out to you?
Can you feel how angry the author must be when this happens?

Anthology and Variations

How I Got to Be a Writer
James Rubin, 3

It makes me really mad when Barbara Danish talks too much. When she talks too much I turn green. Smoke starts puffing out of my green head. I want to dump her in a polluted lake and then bury her in quicksand, then take her out of the muddy quicksand and she's all muddy. But instead I hold it in and let all the anger out in my very very good great excellent stories.

The Maddest Day of My Life
Adriel Reyes, 4

One day on a Saturday I was watching TV and my niece came in. Ohhhh boy, she got me mad. Do you know what she did? She stood right smack in the middle of the TV set. I told her to go to the kitchen. She said, "I am not hungry!" Then I said, "Go play!" She said, "I want your doll." I said, "Go play with your doll!" "I want your doll to be my doll's brother."
So I gave it to her. Then she goes out the door; then she turns around and says to the reader, "Bye, bye. Oh—why don't you come with me?"
Come on, reader, don't leave yet, don't leave with her, please!

Mad. Mad. Mad.
Anibal J. Del Valle, 4

When I'm mad my eyes look like they are on fire,
that a high fever is coming, to 1000°.
I feel like a frying pan.
My hand feels like punching someone
and throwing him on the floor
and stepping on his face until I feel like stopping
which is mostly never.

I Am a Lion!
Betsy Vasquez, 5

When I get mad I feel like a lion that is getting ready to jump on somebody, especially when my brother bothers me. I feel like jumping on him and peeling his skin off and then biting him so hard that he will have my teeth marks on him for the rest of his life, and never forget who did it.

Variation:
When you are angry, what does it feel like inside you? Think of a time you felt this way.

136

In My Room
Maria Molina, 4

In my room I lie on my bed.
When I feel mad I think about what makes me mad.
I feel that blood is all over the walls.
I feel that a person is coming toward me.
Like he is going to kill me.I feel that people are watching me.
The people lock the door so I can't get out.
I see dead people looking at me.
I say, what will happen next?

Miserable Old Me
Lily Chin, 4

One day I feel miserable because every time I ask my mother if I can take a walk, she lets me go. When I walk, it happens. Everything falls down on me and I run straight home as fast as I can and my heart pounds like someone is stepping on me. It sounds like a drum beating. Then I never come out again.

Later, when it was spring, I saw beautiful flowers. I forgot that I was miserable, so I went to my backyard and picked some. Then I thought about everything falling on me. I tip-toed to pick the flowers. Nothing fell. Then I closed my hand around the stems, and then "boom" something fell. I tore out the flowers and I ran back into the house. That was close. My stomach felt like everything was falling on me. I said to myself, "It is going to be a miserable day. "

My Death
Janette Batista, 4

Once I was seeing television. My sister told a lie to my mother and my mother sent me to bed. I was miserable. I felt like stabbing myself. I felt not accepted in my family. I was wishing that I was stabbed but I couldn't stab myself because I felt sorry and upset. I felt like rocks were coming at me. I was scared and I was mad because I had to turn off the light. I felt like killing my sister, too, but when she came to the room to laugh I scared her and she ran out of the room fast.

The next day everyone went away. I was sorry for myself, but when they came back I felt like they were smacking me and punching me and pulling my hair. I felt they were putting me in the cemetery and hitting me with axes and stepping on me and letting the walls fall on me. I was scared because all of the things were falling on me.

The next day I looked at the roof and it was okay.

Michael Williams, 1

One day when I was smaller
I was not big
Mom was mad.
Off to bed.
The baby is bad.

WHAT MAKES YOU ANGRY: EMOTION

A Touch of Spring
Amparo Calero, 4

When I go to the park in spring, I feel happy.
Inside my stomach it feels like leaves
swishing around, and I laugh.
When my mother asks me why I'm laughing,
I say, just a touch of spring
and it feels like squirrels
running to the trees
and butterflies floating around.
I feel like skipping.
Sometimes when I play with my sister,
we giggle alot.

SAYING GOODBYE: VOICE

Father
Charlie Brown, 1

> Dear father, do you remember
> when you put me to bed
> and I did not go to sleep
> and when I cried
> you came and got me
> and took me to the living room
> and put me on the couch
> and you read me a book
> and before long, I fell asleep.

Generating Material/Gathering Details

The kind and amount of sharing will depend on the age of the student. Older students may feel reluctant to talk about separations. For them the introduction and questions can serve as a quiet time for thought, followed by writing.

I ask younger students a simpler question: Is there a person or animal or object that is gone now that you want to say goodbye to?

Ask questions to help students find the details behind their feelings.

Sometimes we don't get a chance to say goodbye to things or people we are separated from. For a few minutes think about people, friends, relatives, enemies, and objects that you have been separated from by death or time or space. Maybe the separation was a happy one. Maybe it was unhappy. Maybe it was someone or something you lost or left behind, or someone or something that lost or left you. Maybe it was a separation that was funny or exciting or sad.

Can some of you share who or what you are thinking of?

Think about the person or thing you are going to say goodbye to, and think about how the separation occurred. How do you feel about it now? Are there memories you have about you and this person or object? Is there something you want to explain to this person or object? Do you have an apology to make? A demand? A question? A message?

You say your cat left? When did you notice it was gone? What did you think? How did you feel? How did you know you were sad?

Stating the Topic

Take this time to say goodbye to the person or animal or object that is your subject. Feel free to tell them whatever you need or want to tell them. You might remember times you spent with them, what those times were like. You might want to ask them a question, make an apology, explain something to them. You might want to say how you think of them now.

Don't worry about spelling or grammar. Concentrate on saying goodbye.

Writing

If students are upset by this assignment or have not lost anyone or anything, give them the option of writing to someone for

SAYING GOODBYE: VOICE

another reason—to say
hello, for example, or to
say welcome.

Sharing

   Have students take turns
reading their pieces aloud
or read them yourself.

Is there a detail in this poem that really stands out to you?

Anthology and Variations

**Goodbye Great Great
Great Grandma**
Kareem Hood, 1

Good-bye great great great grandma.
You were so good to me
when you used to say
"If you be bad I'll hang you on the window!
in the cold! in the night!"
But my grandma did not mean that.
Until, when you were sleeping—
I'm sorry you died.

So you were buried under the ground
in any place in the world
in the deep, in the dirt
and in the devil's home.

But I tried to save you from the sleeping.
But your daughter said, "Do not wake her."
So you died, good bye, and I felt sad.

Lohania Douglas, 1

I went to the river
to see the fish
swimming around in the water.
I saw them going around and around.
I was thinking about my daddy.
I was by myself.
I wondered why I was by myself.
I felt very sad and alone.

Train
Otis Mitchell, 1

Dear little train, I never forgot your broken track.
I remember that you were going fast
and I tried to catch you, but I lost you.
I was sad. I looked in the bathroom
but did not find you. Please come back to me!
I'll fix your track. Okay, pal?

Variation:
Talk to something that
can't talk back.

My Dog Tootsie
Wendy Clinger, 3

Sometimes I wish we didn't have you
and sometimes I'm glad
and sometimes I want to change your name
but you're just a dog
and you can't help it you howl all night
and I can't sleep.
But be careful.
A lot of dogs are getting killed
in the trailer court
by getting out in the road.

Ducks
Rodney Herb, 3

Ducks, I wish you would not use the bathroom
on the place where we park our cars.
Because my Dad does not like it.
My mom does not like it.
I do not like it.
It's a task washing it off.
It's just terrible.

Gary Martin, 2

To animals around the country:
The animal that I like best is a goat
because the baby goats are quiet.

ODES: COMPARISON

To My Earrings
Liza Polaco, 3

You are like a beautiful golden sunbeam
but I would rather have you instead.
You are like a big bowl of gold
but I love you better than gold.
Why?
Because you have gone
through my whole life with me.

Generating Material/Gathering Details

Break the object into parts in order to find comparisons.

When we compare two things we see how one thing reminds us of another. For example, look at these scissors. Can you tell us one thing about these scissors?

You say they open and close? A lot of things open and close. When you look at these scissors opening and closing, do they remind you of something else?

Ask for more information to help the student extend the comparison so it is precise and vivid.

Ah, a set of teeth? Tell us more about those teeth? Whose are they? Why are they opening and closing?

One person thought these scissors opened and closed like a set of teeth. Does someone see them in a different way? Like something very huge that opens and closes, for example?

The fact that they open and close is just one thing about these scissors. Do you notice anything else about them? That they're sharp, metal, etc.?

Practice finding and extending comparisons with objects of various qualities: scissors, ball, paper, etc. (For older students: school, locker, etc.)

Generate a range of ideas so students can find subjects.

Now I'd like you to think of an object you either like or dislike, one you would like to write to. It might be a toy, a machine, a piece of jewelry, a radiator. What are some objects you are thinking of?

Choose one of these objects or another that you've thought of for your subject.

You are going to write an ode to this object and tell this object about itself: its parts and what they remind you of. We are going to use comparison to do this, just as we did with the scissors. If you'd like, tell your object how you feel about it. For example, "Scissors, you scare me when you snap open and shut like a hungry mouth." Ask it questions: "Scissors, do you like the way you click? Do you feel like a traffic light changing?" Give it orders: "Scissors, come with me. We have playing to do."

Have several students address their objects using comparison. Ask questions to help them see the object in parts and to extend their comparisons.

Who wants to share with us the object they are going to write to?
What are you going to tell the mustard you notice about it?
Can you think of something that's as yellow as your mustard?
Look at that sun in your mind. Can you tell us something more about it?

142

Stating the Topic

Get a picture of your object in your mind. See its parts. When you have them in mind, start writing to this object. You might want to make a lot of comparisons or spend all your time on one.

Don't worry about grammar or spelling or punctuation or handwriting. Concentrate on writing to your object.

Writing

Make sure every student has a subject. Ask questions to help them see their object in parts and to extend their comparisons.

Sharing

Have students take turns reading their pieces aloud or read them yourself.

Is there a comparison that really stands out to you?
Does the author like or dislike this object? What comparison tells you?

Anthology and Variations

Braces
Adena Schwartz, 4

I hate you teeth. I need braces because of you.
Braces are so disgusting and terrible.
Everyone is going to call me metal mouth
and steel teeth and I do not want people to do that.
Braces are terrible.
I will look like a quarter of a robot.
Braces look like the city with all metal buildings
which is like a giant's whole mouth
with braces all over his mouth. Braces. Ugh.
Disgusting. Terrible. Absolutely nauseating. Gross.

Ode to My Daily Report
Joe Distefano, 8

Being on Daily Report is like
being a dog on a leash.
Like Alice in Wonderland—
One mistake and off with your head
Like a little person following
you around, waiting
to rat out on all your bad deeds.
Like a man in blue waiting
to slap the cuffs on you.
Like a guillotine waiting for the first
time you get in trouble.

143

ODES: COMPARISON

Clock
Pam Geller, 8

You old clock in room 23.
You confuse everyone.
Just like a teacher who talks and talks
but doesn't really say anything.
Your hands go backwards and forwards
then stop,
until another three minutes pass.
You trick everyone, like a magician
tricks his audience into believing
his tricks are impossible.
When we all think it is time to leave class,
you decide to make your hands go backwards,
and then we have to wait longer.

A Ball Is Like...
Tammi Marlowe,
Alohna Lawrence, 3

A ball is like the center of your eye
or the great moon in the sky, or a balloon.
A ball is like a wheel
or the top of a flashlight or when you say "oh!"
Your mouth looks like a ball.

An Ode to My Radiator
Walt Weisman, 3

My radiator is as warm as a campfire in the woods.
My radiator's steam smells just like dew
after a gentle rain.
It feels like a hard chair but very comfortable.
Its clicks and sputters sound like a bird
in the early morning.

Variation:
Look at an object and let it
set off a chain of
comparisons.

When I Look out the Window
Felicia Rivera, 6

When I look out the window
I see the light blue of the sky blend into a lighter blue
with fluffy cotton candy as clouds.
It reminds me of the sea,
Dark blue, with the sun trinkling on it while setting.
The sea gulls flying over the sunset,
Suddenly a sea breeze with a little bit of ocean air
comes blowing through my hair.
The smell of salt water whirls in my head
like perfume does when first put on.

When I Look at the Blackboard
Javier Elias, 6

When I look at the blackboard on the closet
that has white spots on it,
it looks like a universe that has the chicken pox.
And those chicken pox look like a map
that has spots.
Those spots on the map
look like thousands of islands in the sea
that I can see from an airplane.
Those thousand islands I can see from an airplane
look like a bumpy road full of rocks.
When a car passes on that
bumpy road full of rocks
the tires of the car seem like
they are throwing rocks all around the road.
Those flying rocks look like many meteors
charging down to earth.

Variation:
Compare a person or an animal you love to other things that you love.

To Ryan
Robert Ruiz, 3

You are like a tiger who roars to me.
You are like a bird who sings to me.
You are like a moon who lights me up at midnight
and sings in the beautiful air.
And when you sing to me
my cat starts to dance
and my dog goes crazy
and my bird gets strong.

Chicken and Rice
Olga Marrero, 4

Chicken, I love you
because when I eat you
you are like crackly fire burning
and make me think of biting
into a juicy grapefruit.
I do not like you alone.
I like you with rice.
Rice, you make me think of the blue sky
and flakes you make me think of
white white paper.
But I do not like you alone either.
I like you with salad.
Salad, you remind me
of a juicy orange, just squeezed.

ODES: COMPARISON

To Myself
Jason Tanzer, 5

To myself whose mind is in total darkness in space during a poem:
My mind is spinning, spinning, spinning, and rocks crashing into me.
My mind stinging during my valuable time in writing.

José Ruiz, 3

When Valentine's Day comes you will find something in your pocket.
It will be very special and surprising to you.
I will look at you all day as if I was spying on you.

TALKING ABOUT THE INTANGIBLE

Stomach Flowers
Joseph Watson, 3

When I want to talk
It feels like a pin is poking me.
When I don't it feels like a pencil
sticks in my throat, blocking the words.
I swallow the words and they bloom.
It feels like a flower is in my stomach.

Generating Material/Gathering Details

Any state of mind can be substituted.

Try to remember how you feel when you are supposed to be quiet but you really want to talk. Maybe this happens at home or in school, at a meeting or religious service.

Have students focus on the feeling.

Imagine you have that feeling right now. Pay attention to that feeling of wanting to talk but having to keep quiet. Listen to it. What is inside you causing all this excitement, making you want to talk?

Help generate a range of ideas by asking for various comparisons.
Help students extend their comparisons

Does someone want to tell us what their excitement is? Maybe it is a noise, or something very small or huge, something that is usually harmless.

You say it feels like a time bomb is inside you. Pay attention to that time bomb inside you. Can you tell us more about it? How it looks, the noise it is making.

Help students enter the image and make it real.

Imagine that what your excitement feels like is really inside you. There really is a time bomb inside you.

Do you want to do something to change that excitement so that you won't talk? Something to get rid of the time bomb? What do you want to do?

Have as many students as time allows share their ideas to generate excitement and make the concept of comparison clear.

Is there someone who feels that something different is making them want to talk?

Stating the Topic

Now you get a chance to describe what seems to be inside you when you want to talk but are supposed to be quiet. Go to your feeling. See exactly what's there. What's going on? Write it so we can see it too.

Writing

If students are feeling something very different from this state, let them describe what they are feeling.
If some students use a memory rather than a comparison, let them follow their inclination.

Sharing

Have students take turns reading their pieces aloud or read them yourself.

Is there a detail that stands out to you?

Can you imagine how hard it is for the author not to talk, with something like this inside her/him?

Anthology and Variations

When I'm Talking
Musa Moore, 2

It feels like little people sitting in their chairs
and laughing in their chairs.
When my mother comes in they jump in the closet
and then I get quiet.

I Want to Talk
Chyvonne Barret, 3

I can't talk when I want to talk.
I was in my house and they were having a meeting.
I sat down and started to talk.
My mother said to stop talking.
I kept talking and talking.
Nobody can stop me.

Thunderstorm
Sherna Safford, 2

A thunderstorm is inside of me.
Whenever I want to scream
I start thundering
and lightning strikes me in the chest.
I scream and yell, Mommy! Mommy!
I want Mommy! and I am thundering,
Help! Help! Mommy!
Mommy get me out of this stupid jail.
She rescues me and I am safe and sound.

Variation:
What does it feel like inside your mind when you have an idea, then lose it?

It Just Goes Blank
Sherrisse Monique Finly, 4

I was in a play. It was called "Snow White and the Seven Dwarfs." I was Snow White and I had to introduce the show. Everybody was clapping for me. First I was so happy, and then everybody stopped clapping and then I just forgot my part. I was scared and embarrassed in front of everybody. My mind just went blank and I was so scared I was just moving and shivering and I just wanted to run away but I didn't want to embarrass myself any more. All the lights were on me, but they were shining in my eyes. I couldn't see hardly anything. All I had to say was, "This play is about Snow White and the seven dwarfs," and say, "On with the show," but the lights were in my eyes. I was steadily looking at the lights, and my mind went blank, and I covered my face. I tried to find my director. I told someone to find the director to tell me my part.

My Great Story
Michael Plantamura, 4

I had all the ideas I could think of and I lost them. I went nuts. I was in my room crying. I can't stand it. I can't. But I got an idea. I went out to the living room. I got a jar that had worms in it and I put my new idea in it. I went to get a piece of paper. When I got back my words were gone.

I ran back to my room. No sign. I looked in the fridge. No sign. I said, they could be anywhere, because I had air holes in the bottle so the worms could breathe.

I went to my room because I was convinced the words were gone. I cried and cried and cried. Then I heard a knock on the door. It was my words. They said, "We're sorry," to me.

"Me too."

"Me three."

"Me four." And I wrote an exciting story. I owed it to those words. I had a great story, just like the one I am reading to my class. Barbara loved my story. I put it in a frame and hung it up. It was the best, best story I ever wrote.

Reinaldo Lizardi, 3

When I can't think I feel
like somebody is painting up and down
with the brush and my eyes
follow the brush up and down
and then when they stop I get dizzy
so I lie down and rest for a while
until it goes away and then
I think about classwork.

I will drag the painters out of my house and say
I don't want any painting in my house!

Variation:
What does it feel like inside your mind when you are writing?

Ebonya Falu, 1

In my mind I feel like a pencil
is running around telling me what to do.
It is telling me, do this, do that,

149

do this, do that.
When I stop writing,
my mind stops talking.

Revenya Mitchell, 1

When I am writing
in my mind I see a lion.
But I don't really see one.
Then I see a light
and it shines in my face.
Then I see glasses
and I put them on.
Then I see a lamp
and I cut it on.
And then I see the lion.

Robert Culver, 3

When I write I feel like I'm in a war.
I have all removers.
I see airplanes dropping thoughts.
And tanks waiting for the big story.
Jeeps shooting crazy with all the things
I could write,
waiting to win the story.
I write submarines blowing up all bad thoughts.
Airplanes crashing in the sea
with top secret dreams that only I know.
And with all this thinking, I finally win.

Jamie Brockington, 4

When you get the idea you keep it in your mind.
You just keep it in and you don't write it on the paper.
You are smiling because you have it in your mind.
Then you start writing and it feels just like a story
you wrote before,
and it feels great when you write your story
and you do your best on every story.
You write very well.
You are very happy when you get a compliment
and you feel good to know that you write well
and you have a nice day with that same compliment in your mind.

Otis Mitchell, 1

When I write a poem
I feel words coming inside me.
Then I write the word.
I try to get an answer.
My self tells me what to put.
My self tells me the right answer.
And I keep going.
Then I think of another word.
On and on I write.

Kareem Hood, 1

I like poems
because they are easy to do.
I think they're fun
but I also love making them.
I feel proud about it.
Making poems is superb,
cooking up a storm
and a whirlpool.
So stick around with me
cool breeze.

Natasha Johnson, 1

When I want to write something
I take my time doing it.
And when I finish my poems
I do another one.
Each morning, each afternoon
and each evening and midnight
I do poems too,
and week after week I do poems.
Forever and forever I will be a writer.

**What Should I Write
About?**
Lisa Daniels, 8

I'm sitting here in this classroom listening to everybody saying "What should I write about?" But I don't know what I should write about either. I'm tapping my pencil on the desk and thinking; but how can I think with this noise level. Most people are starting to get their ideas now so maybe it will start getting quiet!

Even in the silence I can't think of anything to write about. I'm staring at the ceiling and can almost hear my brain ticking away but I don't see a light bulb yet and I'm waiting patiently but I need an idea. Tapping my foot on the floor I'm thinking and thinking and I still don't know. I'm closing my eyes and thinking and here comes an Idea...and there it goes! I see most people reading what they've written so far. Their eyes are going back and forth, like a typewriter. Now they're writing. Their pens are moving across the page as if running away from something. I'm biting my nails, that always helps (it helps my brain but not my nails). That didn't take too long because I had short nails in the first place!

I wish I could put an idea in my head like when you put a tape into a stereo. I'm looking at the window, it's like looking through a magic glass at the beauty of the outdoors. Hey! Maybe I'll write about that...Na! It's nice to look at but not a good topic to write about.

OUCH!!!!! My foot fell asleep!!! I can feel the pins and needles. I'm tapping it but it's still asleep (and everybody's staring at me)! I'm walking around the room but it won't wake up! Doesn't it know it's not supposed to sleep in school! Why can't it sleep when the rest of me is sleeping!! It's starting to go away now (pretty short nap) but, now to get back on the topic. Should I write about dogs, or foods, or books, or what? Everytime my mind gets an Idea it seems to be stamping a REJECT on it and sending it away.

Everybody's exchanging their papers and saying to each other (after they've read it) "That's good," or "That's really good, why can't I come up wtih an idea like that" (I always say the second one)!

I'm tapping my pencil on the desk, now the desk looks like it has black chicken pox! I'm staring at the blackboard but I don't see an Idea, all I see is green! Help!!! I Need An Idea!!! Now!!! How about writing about plants! Yeh, I'll write about plants!! Oh no, I see little hands in my mind!! What are they doing...No...Don't...They're picking up what looks like a plant—but what next...They're throwing it!...It crashed on the floor of my mind—Ow!—That smarts!...Oh well, at least I had a smashing idea for a little while!! Bad joke!!!! I still can't think of anything to write about, but how can I when I keep seeing a book opened to a blank page with my name on it and it says, "There's where she was supposed to put her story, but she couldn't think of what to write about!!!"

INVENTING THE UNEXPECTED

The Big Piece of Lead
David Rosado, 4

Everyday I look at this big piece of lead. But one day it turned into a big monster and started shooting bullets of pencil lead, killing, crushing and destroying, and it could make the lead hot and sticky.

They called the Air Force. They got caught in the hot, sticky lead.

They called the Army to shoot the monster hundreds of times and nothing happened.

Then I had an idea. I started making giant erasers. I packed the erasers and went to an army base. I stabbed two guards and stole a tank. I filled it with erasers instead of bullets. I went after the monster. I shot erasers at him and started for his face. He started erasing, so I called everybody I knew and asked them for erasers after the tank was empty. I got the erasers and before all the erasers were shot, the monster disappeared, because a certain person was smart.

Generating Material/Gathering Details

Something strange happened to me this morning. Every morning, without fail, I get up and drink some orange juice. This morning I went to the refrigerator like I always do. I opened the door of the refrigerator and there—was a cat. That cat opened one eye and said to me, "Would you mind closing the door? I'm trying to sleep."

I'm not kidding. You can laugh. It didn't happen to you. Then I went to wash my face. I can't think of a morning in the last two years when I haven't washed my face. I took the soap, scrubbed, rinsed, and when I looked up at the mirror my face was gone and another face was there! Quickly I splashed cold water on my face and found my old one again.

Emphasize the fact that this occurrence begins with something they do every day.

Ask questions to elicit details.

I wonder, has something strange happened to you lately? Has something you do all the time, that always turns out the same, suddenly gone completely strange?

Exactly where were you when this happened? When you looked up in the sky did you notice anything strange? When did you notice you were being lifted off the ground? Did any thoughts occur to you? Tell us everything so we can really see what happened.

Generate a range of material. Have as many students as time allows share their adventure.

Did someone have a different kind of experience? Maybe you were inside the house when something turned strange; maybe it was at night or you were with a crowd of people. Maybe you were on your way to school.

Stating the Topic

Sit for a minute and see the beginning of the story you are going to write. Remember, it starts with something you do every day and suddenly something unexpected happens. Are there sounds? Conversation? Smells? Go as crazy as you want as long as there are details!

Don't worry about grammar, spelling or punctuation. Concentrate on telling us everything so we can see what happened to you.

153

Writing

Be sure each student has a topic. Ask, What is one thing you do every day?

Sharing

Have students take turns reading their pieces aloud or read them yourself.

What part of this story did you really like?
Did certain details stand out to you?

Anthology

Mike Fernandez, 1

Last time
when I put down
the cereal
I saw a flower
swim down
in the milk.
He said
holo, chomp
and started
to dance.

Strategy
Christopher Bouknight, 6

I took a shower and the water turned away from me. It was running sideways so I ran to the side and it went straight up. Then I used strategy. I put the water hot as it could be. Suddenly the water turned on me. It was scalding hot. Fast as I could I turned the water off and I sighed in relief. When I got out I had enormous burns.

My Pig
Ida Salcedo, 4

Once I was in Puerto Rico and I went to get my little pig. Then it turned into a big rat because it was pregnant. It got my mother by the neck and I jumped on the rat so my mother wouldn't kill it. Then the rat had four children, two girls and two boys. Then it turned into a little pig again and I was happy.

The Gigantic Flying Pillow
Ayman Dais, 3

One day when I came home from school I had a headache. When I got there I went to rest on my bed. When I put my head on the pillow something funny happened. The pillow told me, "WHY DO YOU KEEP PUTTING YOUR HOT BOILING HEAD ON ME!!!" I told her, "Because my head hurts me." Then the pillow got mad. She was getting bigger, bigger and bigger. It got to be a gigantic pillow. She ripped and got mad at me. She picked me up and threw me as high as the sun. Then I fell down. I didn't fall down to the ground. I fell down and held the pillow, kicked her and ripped her to pieces.

LOOKING FOR BEAUTY

Summer Poem
Karen Marchese, 5

A bird floating in the air
like a piece of cloth not able to land.

A white daffodil, like snowflakes
arranged so neat, when the slightest move
will shatter it.

The dirt like a hunk
of brown, chopped nuts.

Generating Material/Gathering Details

Help students understand the concept of looking at a single thing, of finding a precise word.

A bird floating in the air
like a piece of cloth not able to land.

What did the author see that made her write this image? What exactly did she notice about this bird? She didn't talk about a lot of birds, did she? She looked very hard at one bird.

Rain slides slowly
and drops itself on another.

What did the author see that made her write this image? Have you ever watched a single raindrop slide down a window and drop on another raindrop? Do you think that word *slide* is a good one to use?

Writing is about spending time looking, and looking hard, to see the little things we may not have noticed.

This lesson can be done in the classroom, if students can see snow or rain out the window. It can also be done on city streets if there is no park close by.

Today we're going to go outside and see what we can find. We're not going to look at all the trees; we're going to look at one tree. We're not going to look at all the grass but at one blade of grass.

We think grass is green—but is all grass green? What is the shape of a piece of grass? What are the parts of a piece of grass? How, exactly, does the blade of grass you are looking at move?

Look in strange places for things to see—under the ground, inside bark. Look up close. Look at colors. You might hear a noise. Write down whatever you see and are amazed at. See as though you'd never seen anything before.

Make each thing you see a separate poem. This isn't a story you're writing, remember. It is one small picture, an image.

Writing

If a student *does* look at trees or grass in general but sticks to the intent of the lesson—to see in images, as if looking at something anew—then go with the student's vision. Focusing on the single unit is a way

to help the student see, not
a straitjacket.

Sharing

Have students take turns
reading their pieces aloud
or read them yourself.

What exactly did the author notice? Have you ever noticed that?
Is that verb the most precise one she/he could have used?

Anthology

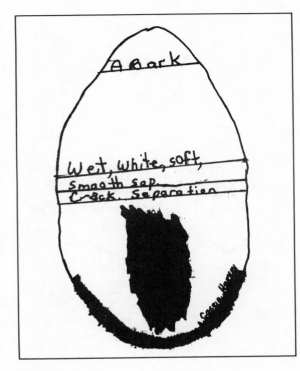

A Bark

Wet, white, soft, smooth sap. Crack. Separation

SQUIRREL

Like a hunter you must get your own food, protect yourself by leaping away from FEAR!

The ocean hitting The rocks— Crystalling a llover

a Star

A black dark sky stars shining brightly diamonds sparkling in the night

Jose Ramos

157

Weed so tall
and I can't see
anything else but weed

Amparo

A group of leaves
FACE each other. When they
Move they talk to each other

Maria
Molina

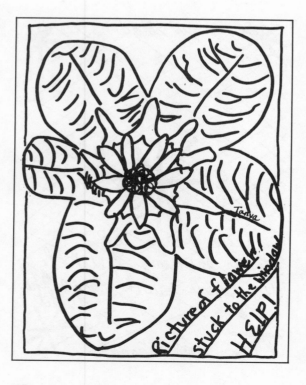

Pictures of flowers
stuck to the window
HELP!

Tanya

In
the
park
the
grass,
very
soft
it
shines
like
glass.

NOTICING THINGS

Observations of an Eighth-Grade Class

> I notice that I'm changing because I used to play a lot but now I'm getting more tired. I feel like I'm in another world. My friends and family try to please me but it doesn't help. I want to tell somebody but I can't.
>
> I got on the train and started to sit down and some old lady with a mop charged for the seat.
>
> I just noticed when I'm alone in my house I feel like crying.
>
> What I notice is that my sister has a boyfriend. Ever since she's had a boyfriend she's been acting all kinds of ways. She was even daydreaming. She always talks about her plans when these two get married. P.S. Her boyfriend's face looks messed up. Everytime people see him they sneer at him.
>
> I notice when I'm quiet I feel very good and when I'm quiet people like to bother me.
>
> I noticed a few days ago I cannot be reasonable with anybody anymore and how it feels to have your feelings hurt by someone you really love a lot.
>
> This morning I saw all the cars pass like a piece of paper instead of being backed up.

Generating Material/Gathering Details

After giving each student a small piece of paper, I write on the board, Things You Notice About Yourself and Other People. You might want to give some examples of your own to provide a range of observation.

We're always noticing things about ourselves and other people. For example, I've noticed that sometimes, if I'm lonely, I wish someone on the street, someone I didn't even know, would take my arm and ask me what was wrong. Last night I noticed a woman who looked like she was going to faint, but when I asked if I could get her a seat she said no.

Take two minutes and on this slip of paper write one or more things you've noticed about yourself or other people. It might be something serious or funny, a thought or an event or a physical feeling. It might be about yourself or someone else getting older or changing.

If you want, you can begin your sentence, "I notice..."

Don't put your names on the slips, and use an X for other people's names.

I collect the slips and then read the slips.

We just got thirty writing ideas simply by jotting down what we've noticed around us. Listen to these ideas and choose a subject for your writing. You might want to use the one you wrote down. Another person's idea might spark a new subject for you. You might even want to use someone else's observation if it's something you've experienced too. Don't worry about copying—if five of us wrote about the same subject, our personal experiences would still make each piece different.

There are several ways you can write about this subject. Let's say your observation is "I notice that when I'm quiet I feel very good and when I'm quiet people like to bother me." You might want to write *about* this, thinking more about it on paper. Or you might *show* what happened that led you to this observation. For example, you might show a time that you were quiet: Where were you? What was going on around you? Who came over to bother you?

159

Have students tell what the writer might have seen or experienced that would lead her or him to this observation.

What were you thinking? Or you might combine the two approaches.

To make these approaches clear, let's look at a few more of your observations.

Stating the Topic

Remember the subject you have chosen. If you're not sure what you want to write about, sit quietly and think about what you've noticed lately about yourself: ways you are changing, things that aggravate or excite you.

Whether you choose to write about your subject or to show what you have noticed, write everything that comes to your mind that has to do with the observation, even if it's not in the right order. Don't worry about grammar. Concentrate on your writing.

Remember, you don't have to share what you write unless you want to, so please write honestly.

Writing

Be sure that each student has a subject.

Help students *show* what they have noticed by asking, "Can you remember one time when you noticed that?"

Sharing

Have students take turns reading their pieces aloud or read them yourself.

Is there one detail that really stands out to you in this piece?

Do you like this way of getting a subject? If you wanted to write but didn't know what to write about, would this method help you find a subject?

Anthology

My Sister's Boyfriend
Lamont Gathers, 8

My sister's boyfriend seems like he never had a girlfriend before. They only became girl and boyfriend with each other two days ago. Yesterday she was so excited about it, she called my cousins Jackie and Pamela. On the phone she told them she had a boyfriend. She described him. She said, "He is a little bigger than me. Just about my complexion, good looking, tough and strong."

I said, "Let me describe him. His face looks like it's been beat up by many people. He's dumb. He's tall. He starts trouble. He's fresh and he's greedy." Sometimes I wish she never went out with him.

Today I was spying on my sister and her boyfriend to see what they were doing. They were talking about their plans for going places together. Then they started playing with each other. I got sore. I popped out of nowhere, surprising them. I said, "Shame on you, going out with a person who's fresh. How dare you?"

She said angrily, "So what? I can go out with any boy, anytime I want to."

I said, "How dare you talk to your big brother like that? I ought to whip you right in front of your prehistoric boyfriend. If y'all grow up and have kids you will abuse them. Look at how snotty you talk to your own family!" Sometimes I wish I didn't have a sister. They are a pain in the neck.

Pain
Carlos Rodriguez, 8

Crazy doggone world, so much looting and killing. People walk right by crime as if they didn't notice what was going on. The sad truth is, they don't want to know what's going on. So much pain and suffering. Why couldn't everyone work together; it's possible, isn't it? I'd really like to get out of this city. Go to a tiny island with enough fruits and vegetables to last a life time. Live with people who wouldn't be so quick tempered, people who wouldn't make others afraid to walk the streets at night. Why can't that dream come true? Why can't I get out of this place?

I really feel mad at this moment, I don't know why. It's just a burst of anger that wants to come out, but it's afraid of the consequences, afraid of what it's going to make—misery, sadness. Pain! I guess pain has something to do with anger. I often look back at the awful times of my life and I realize, my god! Most of them could have been prevented.

Sometimes I go into my room when I'm all alone. I wonder, why was I, out of everyone else, picked to stand up to people, not walk by crime? Why me? I wonder, why me?

**When I'm Alone I Feel
Like Crying**
Lisa Lopez, 8

When I'm alone in my house I feel like crying because there's no one to talk to. I'm in my house in the first room. All the lights are off except a little lamp. Here I am standing next to the window, looking out. I start thinking all kinds of different things, that no one cares about me and what if no one comes back here. They probably will leave me here all alone.

Slowly, my tears begin to come down my face. I wipe them off but more and more tears come down so I say to myself, "I'll put the radio on so I can get cheered up." I move away from the window, put the radio on, then go back to the window. My tears are still coming down. All I'm thinking about is that no one cares about me. No one will ever come back for me. I back away from the window, look in the mirror and I ask myself, "Why are you crying?" I answer back, "I don't know, I just feel like it." And I keep crying for no reason at all.

SNAPSHOTS

Cathy
Elsie Martinez, 8

Cathy Getting Mad
She gives you dirty looks.
Then makes stupid remarks:
"Does anyone have a knife so I can kill
or will scissors do the work?"
Hurting people's feelings when she's mad
is her specialty.

Cathy Getting in Trouble
Fast talker that Cathy is—
But I'm faster.
Defends herself when she's right.
Scolds herself when she's wrong.
Does as she has to to get out of trouble.

Cathy Reading a Book
She holds her book high
listening to all conversations around her.
But somehow she ends up
knowing what she read.

Generating Material/Gathering Details

This is a good lesson for examples. You might want to use the snapshots you wrote in the workbook or the examples that follow this lesson.

Today we're going to look at a person by writing snapshots.

Sometimes when we write a memory it's like a movie: something happens that is caused by something else, and it causes another thing to happen.

That's not what we want to do today. What we are writing today is not a movie or a story but a snapshot—a tightly focused picture, a single event, like a person getting mad, eating, playing a game.

Let's say we're writing a snapshot called Barbara Talking to the Class. What specific things do you notice about me as I talk?

Here are some examples of what I mean. See if you can see these snapshots.

Write the names of some people you know and like.

Now take a look at your list and star the person you'd like to think about some more.

Generate a range of responses by suggesting categories, breaking down, and associating. Remember to get activities that are small enough for a *snapshot*.

As you write these activities on the board, keep reminding students, "We're talking about an action, we're not telling a story."

Keep this person in mind. Now let's brainstorm activities you've seen this person, or anyone else, doing.

You say taking a bath? What are other things you do alone?

You say learning something? There are a lot of things people learn. What are some of them?

You say music? Exactly what having to do with music? Playing an instrument? Singing?

Stating the Topic

Now get ready to write. Listen while I read this list, and see your subject doing one of these activities, one you've actually seen the person engaged in. You might choose an activity that is not up here.

Remember, you are not writing a story. You are merely stopping time and showing, in a few lines, this specific person engaged in this specific daily activity.

Use verbs, similes, conversation—anything you need to make this snapshot. Try a few activities.

Writing

Be sure that every student has a subject. When necessary, ask questions to help students find precise details.

Sharing

Have students take turns reading their pieces aloud or read them yourself.

Is there a detail that really stands out to you? Can you see the subject of the snapshot engaged in this activity?

Anthology

Christine Sleeping
Kevin Anson, 8

Her mother sent me into her room
and she was sleeping on her side. Her
face was wrinkled like a raisin.
Her eyes were closed tight as sealed
windows. Her mouth was wide open,
wide as a cave.

My Brother
Pam Geller, 8

Waking Up

He is very grumpy and cranky when anyone tries to wake him up. He punches and kicks and makes whining noises if you come near him. He thrashes around and hides his head under the covers.

Playing the Piano

He sits on the edge of the bench with loads of confidence which shows on his face. One foot is on a pedal. His hands are gently resting on the keys. His head is leaning forward, carefully studying the music. He begins to play, very slowly, taking long pauses between each note.

John
Albert Chang, 8

John Looking at the Mirror

When you go over to John's house his mother opens the door and tells you that John is in his room. I walk in and I see John in his underwear in front of the mirror making muscles. The mirror looks like it has smog around it. When John tries to look at the three hairs on his face the mirror breaks apart. He thinks he's a Hollywood star when he gets in front of a mirror. He starts to sing, dance, and jump around. One time I saw John practicing something he was going to say to a girl, looking at the mirror.

Waddles
Grace Wilson, 8

Waddles Asleep
During the day Waddles sleeps in the living room.
He sticks up all four paws like a dead horse.
At night he usually sleeps with me.

Waddles Playing with a Tennis Ball
Whenever Waddles gets a tennis ball
he throws it high in the air.
He tries to catch it,
jumping and hopping like a kangaroo.

The Reason for Waddles' Name
He sways from side to side when he walks
like an old tree in the wind.

BUILDING SNAPSHOTS INTO A CHARACTER

Michelle the Brat
Jean Golecki, 8

My sister Michelle is a brat. When she comes home from school, watch out because she is mean and nasty! She gives you a sarcastic answer if you tell her to do something. So now she is in a bad mood for the day. She ignores you, gives you sarcastic remarks and starts arguing over nothing. When she's like that I just ignore her like she ignores me. Now I might say something that she doesn't like. She goes to tell my mother. I say, "I don't care."

Michelle might start a conversation about someone I know better than her. I tell her it's someone else she's talking about and she says, "I know who I'm talking about." Now she's ignoring me again. Michelle hates to be corrected. You can correct her, but she'll get really mad, stomp into her room and of course again she'll ignore everyone.

I walk into her room to look out the window. Then Michelle yells at me and blames me for getting her punished, which I know nothing about. After she's done yelling at me (by then I'm half asleep), she has a screaming fit. She follows me out of her room. By the way, I'm already in the den (which is two rooms away), watching television, not paying any mind to her. When Michelle finally stops yelling and pouting plus whatever else is going on, *I* yell her straight back into her room where she kicks at me (confidentially, she never touches me). I tell her that she bothers me with her stupid remarks and sarcastic answers. We argue and she's losing because I'm ranking her out.

She's a real brat when you ask her nicely to get something for you. She says, "Am I your slave?" When you tell her to forget it, she goes right ahead and does it anyway. Michelle can get you very mad. *I* know!

Generating Material/Gathering Details

Today we're going to write about a person you know well, someone you basically like. We're going to try and get a whole picture of this person, as if we were putting a lot of snapshots together.

Make a list of people you know pretty well and feel basically good about.

Now star the one you'd like to think more about and use for your subject. Keep this person in mind as we go on.

Get a range of possibilities by letting responses suggest categories, by breaking down, and by associating: gesture, dress, voice, habit, expressions, ways people act when other people are around, ways they act when you're alone with them, etc.

Since we're going to write everything we know about this person, let's brainstorm the kinds of things we *can* know about a person, to help us get ideas. For example, how a person speaks, how a person walks, etc.

You say tone of voice? What are different tones of voice?

You say waddle? Are there other specific ways people walk?

BUILDING SNAPSHOTS INTO A CHARACTER

Stating the Topic

Think about the person who is your subject. See the person in your mind. You might not notice clothes at all, but you might be very aware of voice quality and how it changes or of facial expressions. There might be something you really like about this person or something that surprises you. Let these details come out on the paper. Write everything you can think of. Try to see particulars the way we did when we wrote snapshots, but let the snapshots flow together to give a larger picture.

Writing

Sometimes students will make their portraits into memories. That's fine.

It's possible to get bogged down in details that don't add up to a particular person: blue shirt, brown hair, socks. That could be anyone. Ask questions that help direct the students to exploring their particular subject: Are there certain things they like about this person? Little habits the writer has noticed?

Sharing

Have students take turns reading their pieces aloud or read them yourself.

Do you get a picture of this person?
What detail stands out to you?

Anthology

The Friend I Once Knew
Eddie Quetell, 8

It's one day in the summer time, a long, long time ago. A man I once knew, he would give my little friend and me money. We would put the money he gave us together and then go to the candy store and buy a whole bag full of stuff, like toys, bottle poppers, games and most of all candy. We would blow up the bottle by pulling it by the string, Pop! One of them popped out as a plane, the other one popped out similar to a rocket. But that man was extra special, he was my father's friend once; his name was Pedro.

Pedro and my father and I would always meet on Sundays after church at a store on 104 Street next to an old bank. We went to Long Island with my father. I brought my guitar along with me. Sometimes I would play a tune, but when Pedro took that guitar I would hear all of the different songs and melodies from Puerto Rico, the place where they have festivals almost every Sunday.

He passed away about two weeks from the day we left there. They sent a letter to my house. My father was on the bed crying; my mother had her arms around him. I came into the room and found him sitting there with his head down, so I came to him and asked him, "What happened, Dad?" He replied, "Don Pedro passed away."

I walked out of the room slowly and went to my room crying. The next morning my father went to the funeral home and made a card with Pedro's name on it. He said, "I need a box; does anybody have one?" So I gave him mine, where I keep my tools for building models. My father taped the card on the lid of the box and went from building to building, street to street, making a collection so that they could bury him.

I went to his funeral so that I could give my forgiveness. There were two little girls touching his hand. I felt so bad that I ran out of the funeral home crying. I said to myself, "He felt like a father to me." Although I play a lot out, going to work, or going to parties there is still a memory in my heart of a man I once knew, who taught me how to play a guitar, and who showed me the way of happiness. He's in those clouds playing that same guitar staying away from trouble for ever, Don Pedro...

Letter to Kara
Anonymous, 8

Kara, hi! I have to write to you for ten minutes and tell you everything I know and see about you. Well I'll start with your features. You used to have short hair; couldn't do much with it; now it's nice and full of life like a model's hair. Your face has stayed the same, your eyes hazel with specks. It's made you look older as you started to wear make-up. Growing tall, changing your personality. You had habits—biting your nails for no reason, always thinking people were talking about you, thinking about what life was going to be like. Well you're here. You love the guys; you always told me everything. We shared things we wouldn't tell anyone else. During your change period we sort of split apart. You acted in a peculiar way, didn't talk to me as much and flirted with the guys too heavy. You got into trouble constantly and then you came to me when you got into trouble. Well we're back together, close again, the way we were, no one standing in between us, talking and telling our feelings to each other. We're the hysterical twosome, flirting with guys, out to find the world and what it's about, mischievous and into trouble. We've grown a lot since the strain last year. You've changed—more mature, got your head on straight. We're going the rest of the way together. We'll always be there.

CONFLICT

A Friend Who Smokes
Lucy Rodriguez, 8

I have a friend who smokes too much and my mother doesn't let me smoke. Every time I see her she reminds me of a chimney. She runs to me and gives me whatever she is smoking. She wants me to smoke with her but I don't because if my mother catches me I'll really be a dead duck.

I talk to her and tell her to cut down on smoking because it's no good for her health and all she says is "Leave me alone. It's my life. I'll do whatever I want. I'll even shoot myself if I want. You think I'm stupid. I smoke whatever I want."

I don't say anything. She looks at me and I look at her. She gives me a dirty look and all I do is nothing. I feel like punching her right in the face, but I don't. I remember the time my mother told me, "Lucy, you've got to control your temper. You can't go around punching people in the face just because you're mad."

The next day I wake up. I brush my teeth, change my night clothes to my jeans and sweat shirt and I run over to her house. I see her sitting on her doorstep. I say, "I'm sorry," but she won't listen. I feel like just beating her up but I don't. I'm just about ready to leave when she says, "Lucy.

"The only reason I smoke is because I enjoy it and anyway, who cares? My friends do it, why can't I? Besides, it looks fun. Do you know how it is, staying home all day with nothing to do and nobody to talk to and the house is empty with nobody in it but you? Then your friends come along and they all got cigarettes. But the worst part is, then they say, 'Come down so we can have a ball.' And all you got to say is, 'I can't.' That's why I smoke. I don't care about my life. I used to care. Now I don't. I'm sick of doing all the housework while my brother and sister are out all day playing with their friends."

Then I look at her and tell her, "Look, Cindy, let's just be good friends, okay?"

Generating Material/Gathering Details

Most of us have some kind of problem. Some of us have more than one. Some of us have big problems—trouble with a friend or relative, with ourselves or a teacher or the law or our health. Some of us have little problems—little pains, aggravations, silly things. Some problems we've had a long time; some will pass quickly.

What are some problems that are on your mind now or that you've had in the past?

There are at least two ways we can write about a problem. One is to *tell* about it. For example:

My coach always picks on me. I hate it. I don't know why he does it but it makes me mad.

For students who feel comfortable speaking about this subject, help them find a range of categories. The introductory passage suggests quite a few.

For students who are uncomfortable and self-conscious speaking about problems (usually junior high age or older), let them gather ideas by writing. After giving an introduction, ask them to write one problem they have on a piece of paper, anonymously, without using names or other identifying characteristics. Collect these and read them out loud to get a list of subjects.

Another way is to *show* the problem, to put it in a scene and let us see it. For example:

> My coach always picks on me. Yesterday I hit a foul ball and he yelled, "Can't you do better than that?" The next guy didn't hit the ball at all and the coach didn't say anything to him.

Which of these could you really *see*, as if it were happening?

Today we're going to *show* with our writing. We're going to let someone see us in the middle of this problem we have.

Let's try it with a problem one of you suggested. What is or might be a particular time when this happened?

What is the exact place where this problem occurred or might have occurred?

Stating the Topic

You have the problem you're going to work with. Now you're going to show us a particular time when you had that problem. Put yourself in a place: where does it happen? Let us see what is happening. Show us everything you can about it.

Remember, no one has to read this but you, so be as honest as you can be.

Writing

If some students are really resistant to showing a scene, don't grasp the idea of a scene, or naturally begin *thinking on* the problem through writing, let them go with their inclination. There will be other times to work with scenes.

Sharing

Have students take turns reading their pieces aloud or read them yourself.

Can you see this conflict? What details stand out to you?

Anthology

Conversations
Karen Marsirovetere, 8

My mother was washing the dirty clothes down in the basement. I went to the basement and sat on the stairs. My mother had an aggravated look on her face, so I knew she wasn't in a pleasant mood. I was afraid to say anything because I knew she would start yelling at me. She looked at me with a disappointed look and said, "You could help me around the house."

I said, "I didn't know you wanted me to. Why don't you ask me?"

My mother said, "I shouldn't have to ask you." (Throwing the clothes into the washing machine in a very hard way.)

I sat on the steps feeling very guilty, not knowing what else to do. I started to play with my hands. My mother told me, "You and your sisters are old enough to help out around the house."

I said (in a very angry way), "Ma you know just because my sisters are older than me you think I'm just like them."

She said, "It's only when you want to do something that you say that you're the same as they are and you want to be treated like them."

I knew she was right but I wouldn't let her know that. I started to kick my feet into the back of the staircase. My mother was folding the clothes and mumbling to herself and I could tell she was ready to burst out in anger. I started to walk down the stairs very carefully. I knew anything could set her off. I moaned and groaned as I walked down the stairs. It made a kind of racket with the squeaking of the stairs. I knew what I had to do to make my mother happy. I picked up the laundry basket and asked, "What should I do?" She gave me a grin and a smile at the same time. She felt so much better, so I did too.

Fears
William McGill, 8

I have a family problem. My mother is very sick and it's off and on. That makes me sick. I'm always wondering if she's going to die. I feel that way because she has a job now and she comes home sick sometimes. I wonder if I am going to get a phone call when I get home from school saying my mother is in the hospital or is dead. While I'm waiting at home I try to fix the house. After I finish cleaning, I watch television. Then my mother comes home. She sticks the key in the door. I jump up and meet her at the door. She walks in smiling. She says, "Hi, man and Krista." She comes in and looks in the living room and then in the kitchen. She takes off her coat and clothing in her room and puts on her housecoat. She goes in to the kitchen and asks why I didn't take some meat or something out of the freezer to eat. After she takes the meat out she puts some water on the meat and starts cleaning the kitchen and washing the dishes. While she is waiting for the meat to defrost she reads the paper. Then she cooks and eats and goes her separate way. After a while she asks me what happened on "Another World." I tell her and then I go outside.

My Monkey, Harry
Adam Taub, 8

I was sitting on my bed reading *Romeo and Juliet* for my English class while Harry was sitting in the corner smoking pot. He's an addict. Every Tuesday night he has to have a joint or he'll wreck my room. So every Tuesday I bring him two joints. He always offers some to me but I say, "No thanks."

You're probably wondering why I let him in the house. Well, Harry is my pet monkey (a wild one). I got him as a present from my cousin and if I got rid of him my cousin would be upset.

Harry offered me some pot and when I said no thanks he went to my sister's room and offered her some. But that's the least of my problems. My sister said, "Why not?"

It's beginning to get to be a habit. Every Tuesday night Harry sits with my sister and smokes it up. Whenever I try to ask my sister a question about homework on a Tuesday night she starts laughing hysterically. So I decided to give up doing homework on Tuesday nights.

One Tuesday night my sister wanted to go to a dance. I didn't want her to drive while she was small so I offered to drive. She wanted to drive so I just went with her.

On the way there a cop stopped us and said, "Miss are you small?" My sister said, "Of course not!" But the cop had a test, he took out a balloon and if you could fit inside you were small. Well, my sister did and I had to bail her out of jail.

I called Smokers Anonymous and they said I should hide the "cigarettes." So I tried it. Have you ever been tortured by a monkey and a woman!

Finally I got desperate and I took my sister and Harry to a doctor who told them all about pot. They decided to break the habit.

I haven't seen Harry for a few years now. He sends me a letter and a present once in a while. He said that he was adopted by a godfather. Of course, he can't write but he has a translator. Tomorrow I am going to visit him.

I can't believe it. He must be 3'2" and weigh eighty pounds. He's wearing a three piece tan suit and a tan hat. There are five guys standing around like zombies and two girls feeding him spaghetti. He shouts out orders in Italian and people come running (I don't know how he learned Italian).

"That's my monkey," I yell!

My Terrible Report Card
Joseph Oliveri, 8

I'm in homeroom after getting my terrible report card. I am very nervous but I have decided to open it anyway. I did it. It had very ugly red letters all over it. After I saw it I became angered and I was ready to kill all of my teachers. Then I asked a friend to figure out my average. He said "65."

I said, "Oh, no!!!! Now I have to go to summer school."

Then I went to my locker. I suddenly began hitting people. Then when I got to my locker I threw my books in so hard it shook the school.

Then I began my lonely walk home.

My Fortunate Life
Elizabeth Kiernan, 8

My main problems now are my family and school. My parents are always nagging me and my brothers and sisters tease and tattle on me. School isn't that bad, even most of the teachers are nice. It's the homework, reports, tests, and projects that drive me up a wall.

"Ma! I'm going to the movies with my friends and I'll probably be back at 5:00," I said.

"Alright, honey," mother called, "but you better be because your father and I are going out to eat and you have to baby-sit for your brother and sister. Remember when I leave to lock the door, and don't open it to anyone, and don't use the stove, don't let your brother and sister fool around; if anyone is trying to break in call the police immediately, and if there is a fire get out of the house as fast as you can."

I know she says this because she loves us, but I'm in the eighth grade and should know what to do by now when she's gone, also I heard that speech a million times and I'm getting sick of it.

I have to baby-sit for those pests, and don't even get paid or an allowance.

Kenneth my little brother was bothering me. All I said was, "Kenneth, just bug off. I'm trying to do my homework!"

He said, "I'm telling on you when mommy comes home."

"Good, go ahead, I didn't do anything to you," I yelled with frustration.

My sister and I have to share a room. Whenever I want to read or watch television she wants to sleep. When she wants to stay up I want to sleep.

The closet is too small to fit both of our clothes in it. I asked my parents if they could finish up the attic so either she or I can sleep in it. My father said he wasn't going to fix it up right now. He'll probably decide to finish it after I get married.

I like playing sports, softball, basketball, soccer, football and many other of those active games.

My brother who I told you a little about before, is six years old. He hates sports so he draws sometimes. My father thinks he's the greatest artist in the world. In my opinion I think he stinks. Lots of teachers used to say I was great at art, and that I should go to an art school. The art teacher I have now said I should go into art as a career, like making illustrations for magazines, newspapers and children's books. When I told my father he didn't give any encouragement about a career in art. He sent Kenneth to an art school which my brother didn't even like or want to go to.

Getting back to sports, my father bought Kenneth a baseball glove and a Nerf football. Kenneth never even touched them and he had no intention of doing so.

I decided since no one was using the football to go play catch with my friend, Jessie. My brother saw me and started crying bloody murder, like I was about to kill him.

He ran in the house and cried to my father that he was playing with the football and I came over and took it away from him and gave him a hard kick in the stomach. Of course my father believed Kenneth and came running out of the house.

He said, "Leave Kenneth alone, go up to your room and don't come down until you are sorry for what you have done!"

"But . . ."

"Don't give me any buts go up to your room!"

It was hopeless I couldn't do anything, I just went upstairs and read.

Guess what? My father's fixing up this little room next to ours. It will only fit a bed but at least we'll have our own closets and a place to sleep, read, or watch television whenever we want to, knowing that we're not going to disturb each other. He's painting it yellow to give it a bigger effect. I think I should get the bigger room because I'm older but whatever room I get it will be better than what we have now.

My father also bought me a pad with charcoal pencils. I'm having lots of fun drawing with that and I'm getting better.

Softball season is coming and I told my parents that I needed a glove. They bought me one! Finally!

I guess life for me isn't that bad after all. To think that some kids don't have parents that love them or take care of them. Some people don't even have any folks. That's really sad.

I still have disagreements with my parents but. . .I guess. . .I'm pretty lucky.

Donne Kennedy, 8

I am a twelve year old girl.
I am one of the most
inexperienced girls in the world.
I don't wear makeup nor do I tongue
kiss nor do I smoke.
Sometimes when you tell people they
think it's one big joke.
I am different from people I know—
they are always telling me so.
They always tell me about their boyfriends.
Sometimes I think there is no end.
My mother told me at my age she did
not think about boys.
But now girls are like women
and wind boys around their fingers as if
they were little toys.
Sometimes I wish I was born then.
I would not think or care about
having a boyfriend.

ONE TEACHER'S EXPERIENCE WITH WRITING

In developing this book I have conducted many interviews with teachers in order to explore the connection between their own experience with writing and the way they teach their students to write. I believe the process of self-examination is a useful one which can reveal an unconscious set of assumptions that govern our teaching and our attitudes.

The following interview was conducted with Mary Ellen Bosch, an elementary school teacher at P.S. 107 in Brooklyn, New York. She had agreed to do the Writing Lessons in *Writing as a Second Language*, and I asked her to share her experiences with writing before she began to do the exercises. The first part of the interview took place at the end of the 1979-80 school year.

The only experience I ever had in writing was doing English assignments in school, never writing my own feelings. Once in a while I'd try writing my feelings, but I never felt comfortable because I never learned that my words were legitimate as emotional words. They were only legitimate as rational things that carried a message across in a formal kind of way, answering formal questions that were planned ahead of time by the teacher. I didn't even learn to think that I had my own questions—that was something that came very late with me. In college, learning to be a teacher, I was never taught to do that for kids either. I can't even remember lessons on teaching writing to children. That was glossed over. Yes, they should do writing, and there was always the debate over whether you correct the grammar or not when you do creative writing, and that's about as far as it ever got. Nobody ever solved that conflict.

In college I had an excellent teacher for English composition, but she was very strict. Every word you used had to have the proper referral to the antecedent, precedent, and whatever. Basically, we learned the development of a sentence and paragraph and theme. I hated it. I never thought I had an idea that was worth putting down, but of course I don't think that was ever considered important in any class as long as you had the correct grammatical structure. I don't think very many teachers had the experience of personal writing.

Did you know that this element was missing from your education?
No. It never occurred to me that I should be able to express my personal experience in that way, so it never occurred to me that I should be able to do that with children. I had them read a story and do questions and book reports, a summary of the story, that sort of thing, but never in terms of their own thoughts and expressions—"You do writing not for its own sake but because I have to correct your punctuation." I'm stressing their use of action verbs as opposed to verbs of being, *that* sort of writing, and never am I really asking them to write for their ideas, and I'm doing the same thing to them that happened to me. Now I don't even do that. I feel so bad about it that I don't do anything.

In the past we used to sit with a group of kids when there was a problem—for example, a problem of movement in the classroom—and say,

"Look, this is a problem. How do you think we could solve it?" Everybody had a chance to say their ideas about it and then evaluate those ideas. We never thought to put that into writing. Now I see that using writing that way is valid. You don't have to give them writing just so you can check the sentences and punctuation. Give them the opportunity to say out loud what they're thinking, and it's a natural step afterwards to put it in writing.

Now the problem I have as a teacher is, how do I make writing relevant and not just an assignment? There are not many things available in teachers' guides that give you ideas of how to use what's happening in the classroom: how to make the kinds think about it, talk about it, make it their own issue and then write about it. Teachers' guides talk about a sunny day in the park, the best day of my summer—arbitrary topics that *could* be relevant to kids, but they don't tell you how to *make* them relevant. I know I had these same assignments in school, and I felt, "How can I write anything about that?" But in fact, when you sit down and talk with people, you find out how much you have in common with them. What happened to them reminds you of something that happened to you. I find that very helpful for the children, and the right way to do it—I mean, if there is a "right" way to do it—is verbally. I think it has to be done verbally at first.

I think that maybe the reason I can't take a title from the curriculum guide and make it relevant to the children is that I haven't explored it myself first. I can't do that with the children and do it well without thinking about it myself. If I have half an hour free for writing in the classroom, I can't just put a title on the board. I have to prepare as much as I prepare any math or reading lesson.

Do you think that part of the preparation includes your own writing?

On the surface I say no, but I guess I can say that because I haven't really dealt with writing, so I don't know if it would be helpful or not. I think that if I was planning to give them an in-depth writing experience, my personal writing experience would be important to me. But on the surface, just trying to get kids to feel they're comfortable with writing and that it's okay for them to talk about their feelings and then write them, I probably don't have to have a lot of experience writing. I do think it's important to have thought through an experience, asking yourself enough questions to recall the emotions of the time so you know the right kinds of questions to ask to help the kids recall their emotions, too. I don't think you have to write it down.

That's how you can get them talking and then writing down what they've said. How do you help them make that writing stronger?

I don't know if you need to be a writer yourself to do that. Certainly you need to be a person who's read a lot, because then you know whether what you're reading is satisfying or not. You have to know the child, too, because they can't all come out with the elaborate kind of thing that you'd like to have. I think it's important to share that kind of simple writing with the children. They hear a short piece, and maybe one word of that short thing is good, and that's important encouragement for them.

That was something we never got. Only critical feedback. It was never praise, never enjoyment. "You used the wrong word here" or "It's too short" or "It's grammatically incorrect." You get it back with all the red marks and misspellings, but never "I really enjoyed what you wrote, and this a wonderful word" or "This is a fantastic word, and I love this description. I never thought of it that way." That kind of feedback is good, I think.

Before you began to realize that you were perpetuating this kind of teaching with your own students, had it occurred to you that anything was missing?

Well, let's put it this way. I felt I missed out, because anybody who reads a really good author knows they've missed out on something. How come this person can see things in this way and I can't? Is it just that they see this way or that somehow they learned to be able to? When I would read Dickens I'd say, "That's how I feel. How come I couldn't say it before I read it from him?" But I figured, well, that's the genius, you know, and this is the dummy who would never have that kind of feeling or know she had it, anyway. So I felt that writing was a talent beyond me. I can master grammar and correct pronoun referrals and all of that. That's easy to do. Those are rules. Saying something beautiful is not a rule, that's something a talented person does, and I would never be qualified to do it, or teach it, in the classroom. At least now I can see that if you say something out loud first, it puts you on the level of genius: you can *say* what you've seen and felt. Then writing is an extra thing you can do.

Do you think writing can become more than something extra, that it can become another way of thinking about something?

Maybe. It's like talking to a lawyer; they have a way of thinking and talking that really is just within their realm. Yes, you could probably get to the point where you could write offhand.

And once something is on paper, how do you make it better? Do the curricula deal with that?

Never. I've never seen anything in terms of improving what's been written except in terms of grammar. When I was in college, one thing that impressed me in terms of improving writing was that one teacher was a stickler for never using a verb of being: always make every sentence an active sentence with an active verb. When I read something the way I wrote it, a first draft, and then went over it and changed those verbs, I *felt* the dynamics of what was going on, but it was really a struggle. It was really hard work. I'm glad I went through that, because people tell me I write good letters and that I convey my messages well in written form. But that's uncreative writing.

Did you ever feel you could be a creative writer? I don't mean a professional writer, but someone who was comfortable with creative writing?

No. I never even explored that. I really don't think I could be. If I'm going to put the effort out now, I'll put it out for the kids, not for myself. It's too late for me that way.

What if I said that putting out for yourself would be putting out for the kids, that you would see returns that would make it worthwhile?

I don't see the connection, unless—that might be. It just might be. What you're saying is that after a while, your way of thinking becomes your way of writing and the reverse works too. If I write, after a while I'll say things out loud to the kids that help make their writing easier. But I'm not sure that teachers can do all that. I'm really not.

The second part of this interview took place halfway through the fall semester of the 1980-81 school year, after Mary Ellen had completed the Writing Lessons.

Has your writing experience this summer had an effect on your writing with your class this year?

Yes. I've found that I have better questions to ask kids and I'm willing to spend more time helping them think about their experiences before I ask them to write. In one lesson I gave them some suggested beginnings during the discussion, and the kids didn't use my examples, which I was really glad of. There was very little duplication of ideas. I think that before I did my own writing I wouldn't have given them the time to think through their ideas and they would have used my suggestions more. I'm also more patient in letting them think before they write: if they sit there a while before they start it's okay. I'm also more appreciative of smaller endeavors. Before I always felt they could have written more, even if in theory I knew differently. Now I really believe in their own sense of their writing.

After one lesson I showed the papers to another teacher, and she was really impressed with them. I felt really good, and I thought, "Gee, maybe it's working for me."

You felt the kinds of questions you asked were different?

Questions, yes, and also the way I approached the writing was different. Maybe I wasn't as tense, but I don't really know because I wasn't observing myself. There must have been something that made it possible for them not to even want to use my suggestions. I think maybe one big difference is that when I was telling them my story to get the prewriting discussion started, I believed that it could be put into writing and that it would be as good or interesting as the spoken story. I didn't believe that before. I think my confidence in this helped them believe the same thing about their story. Maybe that's what carried over with them, because they didn't see me write; there was only the discussion.

Do you feel you would now want to write whatever story you told?

Yes.

Do you feel it would be the same as the spoken story?

No, but I'm not sure how it would be different. When I am telling a story I have an audience. You know, when I told the kids my story of what I did when I got angry, they all clapped for me and really got into my story, and I responded to them as I was talking. When I'm writing I think I feel the feelings more intensely because they're right there with me; they're not dissipated by the reactions of an audience. Maybe that's part of what makes people nervous about writing—their feelings are in black and white right in front of them, and they have to deal with that. I don't think I would have changed the sequence of the story if I was writing it. Other than that, I don't know how it would have been different. I couldn't know until I wrote it. I assume that it would be different.

That makes me think of your story about digging up the dandelions. Did you know how you were going to write that story before you started?

No, I had no idea. I don't even remember how I wrote it exactly.

I'll read it to you:

"This yard is gigantic. How many yards make this yard? How many little dandelions in a yard of yards, how many big ones? Do they all have the same type of leaf, green and pointy like an oak leaf, smelly like musty paper from a damp basement? How many roots cover this yard's yard? How many minutes in a yard? It is good my sister is here. She complains but she is company. Dig up the roots. They look like parsnips. Is that why I hated parsnips most of my life? They smell funny, too. How much butter do I love? Can I do just one part today? How many days is a yard? Why isn't Michael here to do this, too? It would be over quicker if three worked. My hands are getting yellow and green. It looks like pig slop. So many lives are changed when I dig. So many little things have to find a new home. My legs hurt. It is soft and warm on this earth but my body presses on my legs. If the lawn is nice we won't be able to use it anyway. I'd rather keep a yard of weeds."

I remember. It was in phrases; it was almost like each idea was coming out as I dug up each root. There was something there, a phrase for that root and for that root, that choppy. I felt choppy when I was doing that.

Do you think that choppiness would have come out if you had told the story orally?

No. And that was the essential difference for me in terms of using your workbook: the realization that something had happened to me that I could talk about is also something that I can write about, and I can now make the children believe the same. I want them to feel the experience that I had writing.

What if a teacher said to you, "I don't need to write anything myself in order to work with kids"? What would you say?

To a teacher like that I would say, "Then the important thing in that writing is to correct the punctuation and grammar." They can let the kids do the writing, and they can put a subject on the board and talk about it, but when they go over that writing they're doing it as a grammar lesson and not as a creative writing experience.

There's that much of a gulf between the teacher who has tried writing for herself and the teacher who hasn't?

Yes. I never would have believed that before, because I hadn't written, but it really does make a difference. I have seen teachers who just put a subject on the board and get some very good creative writing, but it must be the exceptional child who's able to do that; it isn't that it's not necessary for the teacher to have writing experience.

The other day I was at a meeting, and what I really wanted to do was to write about sitting in that room, looking at everybody around me. I had never felt that I wanted to put things in writing before. It took me a long time even to be able to say things out loud, because I was raised with the idea I talked too much. I never thought that I would be able to put things on paper, that I would want to read them after I put them down, that what I wrote could have any interest or value or clarity. But now I find that this is true and possible.

Wanting to write happened to me one time before when I was really upset. I was in a classroom about a year ago, and the teacher was horrible. I wanted to get out of the classroom, and I couldn't. So I took a piece of paper and a pencil and just started writing how I felt. I felt I wanted to get as tiny as a mouse and go out a hole, and I kept writing until I finally said, "I wish I was the Incredible Hulk. I would fill up the whole room and break through the class and run away on the beach by the college." And it satisfied me. I got through the class. But the writing I did this summer made me start thinking that I could describe in writing my feelings of myself and my surroundings, and I had never done that before.

Isn't that what you had done during that class?

Yes, but that was when I was under great stress. I didn't know where else to turn, so that's what I did. At this meeting, though, I didn't want to write because I was bored. I wanted to record what was happening; I wanted the experience of recording. It surprised me, and I kind of laughed at myself for feeling that, but for the first time I wanted to put my experience in writing. I didn't even know what I would write. I felt there were many things I could write, and I had never felt that way before. Before I always responded directly to what was being said. I asked a question or answered one or whatever, but I never thought to write or look at all these things in an observing way, from different points of view, like I did when I was freewriting.

There were times when I was freewriting in the book and I felt, "You don't have anything more to say. Now start thinking about it and see what you want to say." When I found myself formulating sentences in my mind, I'd say to myself, "Don't write anything. You're better off to stop." My father used to tell me, "Think about what you're going to say and go over it twice before you say it out loud. If it doesn't sound as good in your mind the second time as it did the first, don't say it at all." So I didn't ever talk very much. Then in college I met someone who would say to me, "What are you thinking?" I used to say, "Nothing." My immediate reaction—nothing—until I realized, finally, that my head wasn't a void. I had to start thinking about what I was thinking about, and I realized that I was thinking a whole lot of things and it was okay to see those things. That was an encouraging environment for me, and this writing was too, in the same way. It's easy to fall back on what you've been taught, or not even to know you're missing something.

There are teachers who are very well intentioned and understanding and sympathetic and sensitive to children, and they would use these techniques if they knew them, but that doesn't happen. I keep believing that there has to be a way to get people who are nineteen and twenty and interested in teaching to think this way from the beginning of their training and not to wait until they have thirty-four children in front of them. That's when they fall back on the ways they've been taught for lack of anything else to do. Of course, what's even more difficult, and what can't be gotten from this book or any class, is the willingness to be honest in front of a person or group of people and say, "Once I was really angry, and this is how I felt, and this is what I did." It's hard to be honest that way.